The Unstoppable Sales^{SM} Prospecting System

How do some sales professionals seem to have a never-ending stream of qualified leads, whereas others need help even to get a meeting? Is it the product they sell, their mastery of LinkedIn or other social platforms, or simply the result of years of experience?

The answer is not so straightforward, despite what many "experts" will say to you. If it were, everyone would be a master at prospecting, when it's quite the opposite. Studies have repeatedly shown that prospecting is one of the most difficult, if not the most challenging, parts of sales. The good news, however, is that when you do master prospecting, you will be an in-demand sales professional with transferable skills that set you apart from your competition and allow you to have the income level you choose.

This book uncovers the methods, skills, and strategies necessary to build your own Unstoppable Sales^{SM} Prospecting system. Unlike any other, this system equips you with the tools to generate a consistent stream of prospects, regardless of your industry, product, or location.

The Unstoppable Sales^{SM} Prospecting System

Earn Attention, Book Meetings,
and Win New Business

Shawn Casemore

Routledge
Taylor & Francis Group

A PRODUCTIVITY PRESS BOOK

Designed cover image: Shutterstock

First published 2026
by Routledge
605 Third Avenue, New York, NY 10158

and by Routledge
4 Park Square, Milton Park, Abingdon, Oxon, OX14 4RN

Routledge is an imprint of the Taylor & Francis Group, an informa business

ISBN: 978-1-032-99496-3 (hbk)
ISBN: 978-1-032-99492-5 (pbk)
ISBN: 978-1-003-60445-7 (ebk)

DOI: 10.4324/9781003604457

Typeset in Garamond
By Apex CoVantage, LLC

Contents

PART TWO   Build Your B2B Prospecting Foundation

PART THREE   Prospecting Strategies to Differentiate from Your Competition

PART FOUR   Prospecting Mastery:
Indirect Methods to Connect with Prospects

PART FIVE   Build Your
Unstoppable Sales℠ Prospecting System

Foreword

There's a hard truth most sales professionals don't want to admit: buyers don't care about you, your company, or your solutions. They don't care about your credentials. They don't care that you've got 15 follow-ups planned. They don't care about your award-winning product. They don't care that your company is family-owned and has been in business for 73 years. And they certainly don't care that you have a killer email subject line.

What they *do* care about is this: themselves.

Prospects want to know: "Do you understand me? Do you respect my time? Will your solution help me achieve my goals more efficiently, effectively, and profitably than I might be able to do on my own? Can you remove risk for our company, and for me and my job? Are you offering something that genuinely makes my life better? And do you care about my success or are you just interested in closing a deal?"

In today's generative AI-powered world where anyone can create fancy presentations, well-written proposals, interactive video demonstrations, and more, the one true differentiator a salesperson has is their ability to care and provide relevant and personal value.

That's why Shawn Casemore's *The Unstoppable Sales^SM Prospecting System* is so important. It delivers the mindset, methods, and momentum that every serious salesperson needs right now.

In my decades of working with and presenting to sales professionals, executives, and entrepreneurs on "How to Get the Meeting No One Else Can," I've preached a simple but powerful truth: being interesting is easy. Being interested takes work.

Shawn doesn't just echo this truth. Rather, he builds a full sales operating system around it.

This book is a wake-up call for anyone clinging to outdated prospecting methods, robotic follow-ups, or "smile and dial" strategies. It's not about manipulating the buyer or grinding through volume. It's about mastering a value-based mindset, which is truly the one thing you can control in any sales meeting or communication.

Shawn gives you that control. He provides a mindset framework and daily sales rituals that shift the power from external scripts to internal systems. He doesn't just tell you *what* to do. Rather, he shows you how to show up, stay relevant, and keep moving forward.

If you've ever used any of my resources, such as the www.IntelEngine.com or www.YouGotIntel.com, you know I'm fanatical about preparation. I believe that every meeting should start with what the other person cares about, not what you want to sell. Sales isn't about scripts. Sales is about insights. And insights come from research, relevance, and real interest.

Shawn's approach reinforces that beautifully. He'll show you how to rewire your mental habits, ask better questions, and approach each interaction as a value exchange rather than a transaction. Whether you're selling to the C-suite or a first-time buyer, relevance wins. Period.

And relevance doesn't happen by accident.

This is what *The Unstoppable Sales^{SM} Prospecting System* gives you: permission to ditch the desperation, a process to build predictable trust, and a playbook to become the kind of salesperson buyers want to talk to and rely upon.

So here's my advice as you begin this book: Don't just read it. Work it. Annotate it. Break it apart. Integrate it with your CRM, your preparation tools, and your follow-ups. Make it your own. Use it to design a sales experience that's rooted in intelligence, fueled by relevance, and built for this new world where every buyer has infinite options but no time to waste.

Because in the end, it's not the loudest voice that wins. It's the smartest, the most relevant, and the most human. And thanks to Shawn Casemore you're about to become that salesperson.

Sam Richter
Hall of Fame Keynote Speaker, Bestselling Author,
Technology Entrepreneur
www.samrichter.com

Acknowledgments

To my wife, Julie, who has always been supportive of everything I do, even if she doesn't fully understand why I do it. To my boys, who inspire me to work harder and be a better father and person.

My thanks to Michael Sinocchi, Publisher at Taylor & Francis. Without his support, this book (and two others before it!) wouldn't exist.

Lastly, thank you to all my clients for your continued belief in my work and your willingness to try new things. Your unwavering confidence and support fuel me to continue digging and sharing new insights and opportunities to increase your sales.

About the Author

Shawn Casemore is a keynote speaker, sales coach, and advisor. He is the Owner and Founder of Casemore and Co. Inc., a global consulting firm, and has worked with organizations such as CN Rail, Tim Hortons, PepsiCo, MNP, Bank of Montreal, and over 200 other leading organizations.

His speaking typically includes over three dozen keynotes each year at major conferences, as well as speaking at sales kick-off meetings for major corporations.

Shawn's publishing includes hundreds of articles in print and online for publications such as *Forbes, Fast Company, Chief Executive, Industry Week, and The Globe and Mail*. He's also written four commercially published books, including his most recent, *The Unstoppable Sales Machine* (Taylor & Francis, 2022) and *The Unstoppable Sales Team* (Taylor & Francis, 2023).

To learn more about Shawn and his work or to arrange to have him speak at your next event, visit www.shawncasemore.com.

Introduction

How do some sales professionals seem to have a never-ending stream of qualified leads, whereas others struggle to even get a meeting? Is it the product they sell, an amazing offer so good that the prospect can't resist, or their mastery of LinkedIn or some other social platform?

After working with thousands of sales professionals for more than a decade, I can tell you that successful prospecting is not the result of these things, despite what many "experts" might suggest. If it was, everyone would be a master prospector, when in fact it's quite the opposite. Studies have repeatedly shown that sales professionals find that prospecting is one of the most difficult components of the sales process. The good news, however, is that when you do master prospecting, you immediately become a highly sought-after sales professional, with transferable skills, that will allow you to have the income level you choose.

In this book, we'll uncover the specific methods, skills, and strategies to build your very own Unstoppable Sales^{SM} Prospecting system. The system, skills, and methods to generate an unstoppable stream of prospects work for any industry, regardless of what you sell or where you live.

My experience tells me that if you picked up this book, you likely would place yourself into one of the three following categories:

1. You are already successful at prospecting and wonder if there are any new strategies out there that would amplify your existing success. If this is you, then read on. This book will share with you modern prospecting strategies and methods that, when combined, will further amplify and accelerate your existing prospecting methods.
2. You are having sporadic success prospecting and are seeking something that creates a steady stream of prospects, with less effort and guesswork on your part. Good news! This book will share with you a systematic method of generating prospects and creating a steady flow, thereby halting the ebbs and flows of prospect success you currently face.
3. You are new to sales and trying to get your first few prospects to get your business or your career off the ground. You are wise to pick this

book up. You are about to uncover a shortcut to generating a steady stream of prospects and skip all the frustration and effort of testing various methods attempting to determine what works.

Regardless of your time in sales, this book offers you proven methods and strategies to generate prospects in any economy, despite prospects being busy, distracted, and extremely sensitive to any outreach that appears to be spammy.

Are you ready to create your Unstoppable Sales^{SM} Prospecting system? If you are, then let's roll up our sleeves, grab a highlighter, notepad or laptop, and dive in. You are only minutes away from increasing the number of prospects you're connecting with. Let's go!

Shawn Casemore
Chatsworth, ON
May 2025

Part One

Successfully Reaching Today's Busy Buyers

Recently, I spoke at a conference for sales professionals on building an Unstoppable Sales^{SM} Machine. During my talk, I asked the audience, mostly seasoned sales professionals from a wide variety of sectors, what was the most challenging part of selling for them. More than 80% of the room said reaching prospects was their greatest challenge. There were other more tactical concerns, like being ghosted and figuring out how to get past email spam filters, but hands down, reaching prospects was the greatest challenge the audience faced.

Do you find it difficult to reach prospects as a sales professional? If you do, you aren't alone. In this book, I'll provide you with a wide variety of methods, processes, and strategies to get in front of your ideal prospects more easily and often.

Sounds good? If so, let's discuss why prospects seem so challenging to reach.

DOI: 10.4324/9781003604457-1

1

Why Are Prospects So Difficult to Reach?

1.1 PROSPECTING TODAY: MULTI-CHANNEL, MULTI-TOUCH, AND MULTIDIMENSIONAL

My first official job in sales was selling new and used cars back in the 90s (yes, I'm that old). Anyone looking to buy a car would invariably wind up at the dealership where I worked at one point or another. There was no Internet, and email use was inconsistent, so the process was simple. A prospect looking for a car would see an ad either in their local newspaper or on television, or hear it on the radio, which would pique their interest. They had two choices if they wanted a General Motors product that we sold. Visit our dealership or a different GM dealership outside our small town. My job was to be ready when it was my turn, and a new prospect (an "up") would arrive in our parking lot or showroom.

As you can tell, no actual prospecting was required. Anyone considering buying a GM product would visit our dealership, where either one of the other sales agents or I would greet them and begin a conversation. The sales process we followed was simple but provided one challenge. Most people who visited the dealership had already met one of the other sales agents. Therefore, they would invariably ask to speak with someone else. The result? I was one of five sales agents walking the floor, which meant every fifth prospect was mine to approach. However, about 50% of these would ask to speak with one of the other agents, meaning I missed my turn. Therefore, I may meet only one or two prospects a day. There were even some days when I met none at all.

Being on the receiving end of taking any prospects available when it was my turn and being paid 100% straight commission was a difficult way to make a living, so I decided to take matters into my own hands. I realized that if I could get "ups" asking for me when they arrived, I would get most of the leads, but making this happen would require taking a different approach than the other sales agents. So I did what any young, hungry, and eager-to-get-paid would do: I began prospecting.

I practiced common car sales prospecting strategies, like calling old leads to introduce myself, which is something many sales reps looking to build their book of business would do. However, I also practiced some not-so-common strategies. One, for instance, included making a flyer on my dot matrix printer (which shows you how long ago this was!), then identifying the neighborhoods that matched the demographic of our typical "ideal buyer," and then walking these neighborhoods to drop off flyers and introduce myself.

I deployed other strategies, like handing out business cards at local events and wearing company-branded apparel at social events, and the results were profound. Within three months of starting these efforts, people began showing up at our store and asking for me directly. Within five months, I was the top salesperson for the month, beating out those who had worked at the dealership for over ten years. Not bad results for a newbie.

I share this story with you because it provides some lessons I learned years ago about prospecting that are just as relevant today.

1. You've got to be crystal clear about who you want to sell to and put all your prospecting efforts into reaching these people. If others show up eager to buy that don't match those criteria, fine, but keep your energy focused on those you want to sell to.
2. You've got to differentiate yourself from everyone else vying for the attention of your ideal prospects if you want the opportunity to earn their attention. Attention is, after all, the first step in your sales process, and without it, no one will ever hear what you have to say.
3. You must avoid getting stuck using one method to prospect. Change is constant, and sticking with one method that is working now may eventually stop working. You need an effective and repeatable system, and your efforts must be to continuously test new prospecting strategies to keep your prospecting fresh and ensure your stream of new prospects never dries up.

As you can tell from my example above, communicating with and selling to prospects in the 90s was straightforward. Compared to today, with many different communication channels and the Internet, things are more complex and arguably more difficult. From the Internet to social media, direct mail to email, and in-person to virtual meetings, everything about how we get in front of our ideal prospects has changed, and technology continues to move the goalposts.

Let me plant this seed as a starting point for your journey to build your Unstoppable Sales^{SM} Prospecting System. Everything about selling has changed, and yet nothing about selling has changed. The reality is that with all our prospects' technology and communication options, they are highly distracted. As a result, to sell today, you must begin by earning the attention of those you seek to sell to.

1.2 ATTENTION IS THE CURRENCY OF SALES SUCCESS

An old saying asks if a tree falls in the forest, does anyone hear it? There are many answers to this age-old question, so here is mine. The reality is that trees fall daily, and neither you nor I hear them. However, if someone were to share with us through social media, email, video, or other channels, a tree was about to fall or had fallen, like the National Christmas Tree in Washington, D.C., that toppled in November 2023, it would earn our attention (and essentially, we would hear it).

News media, for years, has perfected the art of gaining attention to make a sale. For example, have you ever noticed that if the press reports one plane crash, several others follow? The goal in news media is to earn and retain your attention using whatever channel they need to (e.g. radio, television, or YouTube) so that they, in turn, can place products or services in front of you to encourage you to buy. In other words, attention enables them to sell. The more attention a media outlet can gather (i.e., more viewers and more readers), the more interest they get from advertisers who want to put their products and services in front of its viewers, and in turn, the more money they can charge to these advertisers.

What does all of this have to do with prospecting? You need to think like the news media. In other words, your priority when prospecting is to earn and retain the attention of those you want to sell to, the "ideal buyers" of your product or service. If you don't have their attention or can't earn it, then they don't know you exist, you can't build any trust, and they will likely buy from someone else.

Here's what's interesting. The more attention you earn, the greater your prospect will pursue you. You create a perception that you, your products, or your services are the most common, most popular, and most needed solution in the market. In other words, more attention earned, when done correctly, provides you credibility with your ideal buyer.

Let me give you some examples:

Suppose you are considering purchasing a car and suddenly realize there are similar models of that exact vehicle everywhere you look.

You may be planning a vacation to a tropical destination. As you tell others about your intended trip, you may encounter several people who have already visited the exact location (and you didn't know this beforehand).

You are considering installing an above-ground pool in your backyard and suddenly realize how many houses in your neighborhood have one.

You attend a concert (insert your favorite group, artist, or DJ here) and buy a T-shirt with the artist's name on it. You notice how many people have similar T-shirts.

Our attention goes to the things most relevant to us at the time. This is known as the frequency illusion,[1] a cognitive bias in which a person notices a specific concept, word, or product more frequently after recently becoming aware of it.

So, if you are looking for a new commercial insurance policy, a new corporate bank, a new office for rent, or a new piece of equipment, you will notice examples of these (and suppliers of these) everywhere you turn.

At this point, you might think, "But Shawn, earning attention is Marketing's responsibility." I agree with you to a point. Marketing promotes and attempts to draw attention to the company and its products. Still, since your goal is for prospects to connect with YOU, not your co-worker, inside sales, or your competitor, you need to start earning your prospect's attention. Refer to my earlier examples of how the frequency illusion works. If I'm looking to buy a Toyota Rav4, I might notice Rav4s all around me. What draws me to reach out to a sales professional selling Rav4s is when I become aware that they sell Rav4s (i.e., I receive a flyer with their name on it or find them on a YouTube channel talking about Rav4s). In other words, earning attention is so crucial to selling that it's NOT something you should leave up to Marketing.

Later in the book, we'll discuss methods for garnering the attention of your prospects, but for now, know that this is the first step in your prospecting system. You must consistently earn the attention of those you want to sell to.

1.3 REJECTION IS A SIGN THAT YOU ARE ONTO SOMETHING

When earning attention becomes your primary focus for prospecting, you will invariably run into some barriers. Research by firms such as Gartner has suggested that most of a prospect's time before buying is spent doing their research using online sources. These can include visiting websites, reading reviews, checking social media platforms, reviewing emails, etc. The problem this can create for you, however, is that it is much easier to ignore you, unsubscribe from your email, block you, or send you a "STOP" message when connecting with a prospect digitally. Let me give you an example.

Many years ago, I spoke at a franchise owner event, following which a franchisee approached me and said, "We need your help. Our sales are flat, and you have the formula we need." He then explained his situation and what help he presumed he needed. Considering we had both traveled to the event, we agreed to meet virtually two weeks later and even picked a date/time on the spot to connect. I sent him an invitation later that day.

A week before we spoke, I sent him a LinkedIn connection request with a personalized message: "Looking forward to our upcoming discussion, Bob." He didn't accept or acknowledge the message. A few days before we met, I also emailed him a simple message: "Looking forward to speaking on Thursday, Bob, I've re-attached the link for our discussion below." No response.

The morning of our meeting, I sent a simple text message (he had provided his cell number to me when we met) saying, "Bob, I'm looking forward to our virtual meeting today at 10 am." I have yet to receive a response.

When 10 am arrived, I jumped onto Zoom and waited, and waited. Bob was a no-show.

Herein lies the problem you will face. As referenced earlier, your prospects often conduct most of their research on your products or services virtually, requiring zero interaction with a real person. For some, this diminishes the sale to a transaction in their mind, making it much easier for them to dismiss or brush you off. In other words, the continued trend toward using digital means to enable sales means that, as a sales professional, you might begin to feel like you are simply taking orders and not influencing the sale.

In my example above, Bob's reaction is entirely my fault and has nothing to do with Bob. After my initial discussion with Bob, I assumed (and you know what that makes me) that our discussion was enough to convince Bob that investing his time to speak with me would be a good investment. I was wrong. Bob's challenge (which was trying to increase his sales) is something he had been researching before our chance meeting at the franchise event. He likely continued research after hearing me speak, and as a result, as each day passed, the timeliness of my message aligning with his needs became less and less relevant.

What I should have done is presumed that our initial interaction only opened the door, and it was then my job to provide insights, perspectives, and information to Bob that would assist in his likely quest to continue researching how to resolve his flat sales.

My second mistake was that I focused on confirming the call rather than adding value before the call. Following our initial conversation, I should have shared with Bob many valuable tools and resources that would immediately help his situation and reassure him that I had his answers (and that further research wasn't necessary). These might have included an assessment, a relevant book, or video tips to resolve or overcome his challenges (we'll discuss using value to convert a prospect later in the book).

But my biggest mistake was not confirming the meeting day and time while I stood in front of Bob.

With this in mind, let's jump to Chapter 2, which you are likely eager to do – cold outreach. We will discuss transitioning from a pest to someone your prospect welcomes as a guest.

UNSTOPPABLE SALES PROSPECTING SYSTEM ACTION STEP

What have you been doing to earn the attention of your ideal prospects? Take a few minutes to consider how prospects typically find you, and ask yourself, how can I replicate this to generate even more attention?

2

Cold Outreach

The Good, the Bad, the Opportunity

When prospecting and reaching out to cold prospects, you must consider specific factors to remain optimistic about your chances of success.

2.1 THE INITIAL GOAL OF YOUR OUTREACH

When I think back to all the cold calls I've made in my sales career, from selling cars to memberships to metal brackets and professional services, the actual number of calls would be in the thousands, maybe more.

There is only one instance where my cold call didn't land well with the prospect. After speaking at an insurance conference, a gentleman approached me as I left the stage, presented his card, and said, "We need to talk." It's not uncommon, after speaking, that someone wants to connect and discuss how the strategies and methods I share would apply to their situation, so I accepted his card and told him I'd call him Monday morning. Considering he had heard me speak, I presumed this would be a warm call and he'd be waiting for my call.

Monday morning came, and as promised, I called the gentleman's office and asked to speak with him. Here is how the call went:

"Hi, is John there?" I asked.

"Yes, may I ask who is calling?"

"It's Shawn Casemore. We met at the insurance conference last week, and John asked me to call him this morning."

"I'll put you right through," was the response.

DOI: 10.4324/9781003604457-3

Here is how *that* conversation went.

"Hello!?"

"Hi John. It's Shawn Casemore calling. You asked me to call you when we met at the insurance conference last week."

"Who?"

"Shawn Casemore. I spoke at the insurance conference on Secrets to Sell More Policies in Today's Economy, and you approached me, presented your card, and asked me to call you this morning."

"I don't have time for this!"

And with that, John hung up, never to be heard from again.

I share this story for a few reasons. First and foremost, amongst all the calls I've made, this is the only time I have ever had someone hang up. Additionally, you'll note that this call was warm. John had met me briefly and heard me speak, so my name and voice were not foreign to him.

Lastly, the situation demonstrates an essential point about outreach: To connect with prospects, you must earn and retain their attention.

Sticking with John's situation for the moment, considering he ran a small business, it's likely he was knee-deep in all sorts of problems when I called, and reaching out to him on a Monday morning (a typically busy time for anyone) was not likely the best move.

Regardless, this is the only call I can ever think of that left me baffled (at the time) about what had happened. I failed to realize that although John had decided to give me some time after hearing me speak, various distractions consumed his attention, lessening his attention on me.

When reaching out to prospects cold, remember that you are interrupting them, so whatever you say, offer, or suggest had better be relevant, helpful, and timely. In today's highly interconnected world, your prospects are bombarded with messages, meetings, projects, travel, employee issues, customer problems, technology issues, and a host of other priorities, not to mention their priorities.

Attention isn't just handed to you; it must be earned. Once you earn it, you must retain it. Numerous studies over the years have attempted to capture the attention span of a human being, specifically in online media and advertising, and the estimates range from mere seconds to under three minutes.

Let me give you an example. It must be an emergency to capture 100% of someone's attention. For example, if we were in a room and I yelled "Fire!" you would place 100% of your attention on me for a few seconds and then search for an exit while observing the room around you.

Of course, I'm not suggesting you yell "Fire!" at your prospects, but you need to realize that your prospects' attention isn't something you are automatically granted. Moreover, the reasons someone might give you their attention differ by individual.

The work of William Marston,[2] whose research formed the basis for some very popular behavioral assessments, suggested that four predominant behaviors exist in all human beings and that two of these behaviors are highly focused on the task. In contrast, the other two behaviors are highly focused on people. Marston's work provides some clues as to what is required to earn someone's attention; in some instances, benefits to people and teams may earn some prospects' attention, whereas for others, improvements to tasks and productivity may be the priority.

Although Marston sheds some light on how we earn attention, his work also demonstrates just how complex and difficult it can be – unless you have a formula.

2.2 THE PROSPECT ATTENTION FORMULA

Earning attention is part art and part science. In other words, although there is a formula you can use, you'll need to add some of your creativity and be willing to test and trial changes in the formula repeatedly. The main reason for this is that the attention spans of humans are constantly evolving based on societal factors, technology, time of the year, and the like.

Let me give you an example. Suppose you had a decent-sized network on a social platform like LinkedIn during the pandemic, when people were glued to their phones, and you used that platform to reach out to prospects and engage in a discussion. In that case, you could generate a lot of conversations, presuming your network contained relevant prospect connections. Trying to connect with prospects during summer vacation using their office telephone number is less likely to get their attention, as they aren't in the office. If you catch someone in the office on the phone during the often-slower summer months, the chances are that they'll give you their attention by taking your call, due to fewer distractions.

For this reason, you need to consider earning attention from your prospects as having several variables that can shift, sometimes temporarily and other times permanently. Let's look at the basic formula with the most common variables.

Prospect Attention Results from:

A Specific Challenge + Your Unique Solution + Relevant Social Proof + Reinforcing Value

1. **Challenge**: A current issue, challenge, threat, or opportunity your prospect faces that is specific to the problems your product or service has overcome.
2. **Unique Solution**: These are the solutions that your company provides, presented in a way that makes them unique from your competition.
3. **Social Proof**: These are examples of other similar companies you've worked with to resolve these challenges with your unique solution.
4. **Value Assets**: These are the resources, including research, checklists, assessments, free samples, trial periods, demonstrations, etc., that demonstrate your ability to overcome the challenge and cost nothing to the prospect.

Throughout this book, we will refer to the Prospect Attention Formula, adding different elements and components as we build your Unstoppable Sales^{SM} Prospecting System. For now, use the preceding formula and the following questions as a starting point for earning the attention of your prospects. Take a minute now to answer the following questions:

1. What specific challenges or issues do your prospects face? If you are unsure, reach out to existing prospects and customers and ask them about their biggest challenges. Assess how your product or service can address or overcome these challenges.
2. What is unique and different about your product or service that helps to overcome these challenges? How is it different from what your competition offers today? What features or benefits stand out and make your solution unique?
3. What are examples of different customers or clients (in other sectors, regions, or companies) that you've assisted in overcoming these challenges using your products or services? Capture these as testimonials in written, video, and case studies to share with prospects.
4. What free resources do you offer to prospects today (or could you offer) that would assist in addressing part of their challenge or create a pathway toward a solution (that you sell)? These include free samples, trials,

or demonstrations, or they could consist of assessments, checklists, tip sheets, etc. They should vary in format, including written, video, audible, kinesthetic, etc.

The insights from these questions provide a foundation to differentiate yourself, your company, and its products and services from your competition. In other words, you can't just blend in with the carpet if you want to earn attention. If you do, you are at risk of either being ignored, or at best, your prospects will consider you to have an identical offer as your competitors, and as a result, they will assess you and your offer based solely on price.

Is this where you want to be?

When you appear to be the same as your competition, your prospect has no choice but to make a "buy" decision based on price. Specifically, whoever has the lowest price will get their attention, and most likely, it will begin with a negotiation for an even lower price!

Sound familiar?

When it comes to earning the attention of cold prospects, the attention you earn comes in three different forms:

Relevant Attention is the attention we've been discussing. You earn attention by presenting yourself, your company, and its products and services as the best solution for your prospects now and in the future.

Irrelevant Attention is the attention you've gained (not earned) from something unrelated to your prospect. Examples here might be newspaper coverage because of a significant charitable donation or an announcement of your company's expansion in a magazine.

Undesirable Attention is the attention you gain that does not place you in a positive light with your prospects. Examples might include an executive at your company being arrested or your product being recalled.

As you can tell from these examples, not all attention is good attention, despite what some experts suggest. Our goal is to get you relevant attention. We'll leave irrelevant attention to the marketing department and avoid undesirable attention at all costs.

To ensure you gain relevant attention, let's discuss some mistakes that sales professionals can inadvertently make while trying to earn attention. As we review these, do a self-check to assess if this is a mistake you're making and, more importantly, how you can avoid it.

2.3 FIVE ATTENTION-SEEKING MISTAKES TO AVOID

Recognizing that gaining attention is the primary step in your sales process might lead you to jump the gun and start doing crazy things to get attention. As we've discussed, not all attention is good attention, so let's be clear on a few things before you go any further.

There are plenty of methods you can use to earn attention, and some you should avoid. For now, however, let me share a few of the common mistakes I've seen sales professionals make in their attention-seeking outreach that limit their ability to connect and build relationships with their prospects. The goal is to ensure you aren't making these mistakes as a starting point.

1. **Lack of Differentiation**: Your messaging, approach, and language sound like everyone else's. You blend in and are undifferentiated, and as a result, most of your prospects respond only when you can offer a lower price.
2. **Lack of Creativity**: Your methods and strategies for engaging prospects are stale and outdated (e.g., "Let's have lunch"), and as a result, you are irrelevant and uninteresting to prospects (and your response rates show it).
3. **Mono-channel Communications**: You repeatedly use the same communication channels (e.g., email or phone) and don't use a multi-channel approach to engaging with prospects who have their priorities in how they want to engage with you.
4. **Lack of Momentum**: Your outreach schedule and activities are inconsistent. You lose touch with prospects, miss, or don't follow up on inbound messages quickly, and, as a result, lose momentum in moving prospects forward.
5. **No Prospect Journey**: You haven't developed and don't take your prospects on a strategic journey to learn about you, your company, and the unique benefits of your product or service.

2.4 WHY YOUR COLD OUTREACH DOESN'T WORK

Selling is a numbers game. In other words, the more relevant prospects you connect with, the better your chances of making a sale. Your path to quickly building meaningful prospect connections is to be more strategic about how you earn your ideal prospects' attention.

Let's examine a few of the common mistakes that many sales professionals make in their cold outreach to help you earn attention and generate more meaningful prospect conversations.

2.5 COMMON COLD OUTREACH MISTAKES TO AVOID

1. **You aren't personalizing your outreach**. Every prospect you reach out to has a series of current priorities they are dealing with, from business to personal. You might think it's impossible to know what these priorities are, but that's not entirely true.

    Researching BEFORE you reach out to a prospect is critical to ensuring your outreach is personalized.

2. **Your positioning lacks substance**. Selling lemonade on a hot summer day on a busy street corner is likely to result in some sales. Attempting to sell that lemonade amid a snowstorm on a deserted gravel road is unlikely to result in any sales.

    The positioning of your product or service, what you say, and how you say it matters. Effective positioning is how we differentiate and ensure our product or service is viewed as our prospect's best solution or option.

3. **Failure to use referrals**. You may not have a direct referral to a new prospect you are pursuing, but you likely have some connections you can reference. LinkedIn is an excellent resource for viewing who you both know, which can lead to a direct introduction or some relevant name-dropping.

    Connect outreach with a mutual relationship, either current or past, that can break down the initial barrier of not knowing you.

4. **Lack of effort**. Suppose you repeatedly cut and paste messages into email or social media messages or use the same script for your outbound calls. In that case, your prospecting is not as effective as possible.

    Although there are common characteristics, challenges, and circumstances among your prospects, each prospect you attempt to connect with is a unique individual. Therefore, you need to invest some time learning about each prospect before you try to communicate with them.

5. **Unwillingness to learn**. If you picked up this book, then it's unlikely this is something you need to worry about. However, periodically, I meet sales professionals, business owners, and even sales executives who are confident they know it all when it comes to prospecting and sales in general.

Let me also point out some things that might not be obvious in this list. We rarely discuss whether cold calling (using the phone, for example) is effective or ineffective. I also don't discuss sending cold emails or cold messages. Truth be told, they can all be effective if you use them correctly. We'll discuss how shortly; however, for now, recognize that becoming unstoppable in your prospecting requires you to focus your time and efforts on continuously earning the attention of your ideal prospects. So, as the economy changes, technology changes, and your prospect's priorities change, the methods, messages, and value you share to earn attention also need to change.

Before we move on, let me reassure you that we'll dive more into using these various methods in your outreach shortly. For now, I just want you to think about what you say and how you say it to your ideal prospects. That's how you earn attention, and once you master this skill, your outreach, however you choose to do so, will be much more effective.

UNSTOPPABLE SALES PROSPECTING SYSTEM ACTION STEP

Top-performing sales professionals are always on the lookout for new ideas, new strategies, and ways to earn the attention of and connect with their ideal prospects. They don't rely on past success. What strategies have you considered and not yet tested? How quickly can you test these strategies out to know what works and what doesn't?

3

Warming Up Your Cold Outreach

Many sales professionals think that selling is a numbers game. It is, however, charging forward with the idea that the more emails you send or calls you make, the more sales you generate is a misnomer. The fundamental objective in selling is to ensure that your outreach, interactions, and conversations mean something to those you interact with. The more meaningful you can make each conversation with a prospect, the greater your opportunity to sell.

Let's start with the biggest challenge for any sales professional when generating meaningful interactions. Prospects aren't lining up to speak with you. They don't even know you exist, so your starting point is to answer one crucial question. How can you connect in an impactful way that earns their attention and leaves them interested in learning more about you and how you might help?

The answer to this question varies depending on various factors, so for now, let's discuss connecting with cold prospects. In doing so, we'll presume you don't have a marketing department handing you a list of warm, qualified leads they have vetted or strangers repeatedly reaching out and begging you to take their money.

3.1 SLOW DOWN YOUR OUTREACH TO SPEED UP YOUR CONNECTIONS

A couple of years ago, I was scrolling online looking for an awning for our deck. The sun faces our deck, so in the summer months, sitting out between 11 am and 4 pm can become almost unbearable unless you enjoy sitting in 90-degree sun, which I don't. I came across an ad for a power awning, and

DOI: 10.4324/9781003604457-4

after some further research, I realized it was sold by a company that was only two hours from my home.

The awning seemed like a good option, and the fact that it was powered was a benefit, considering we needed an awning that was quite large, about 12′ × 20′. Unfortunately, I couldn't find pricing on the website anywhere to get a sense of whether this was within our budget, and considering it was the weekend, I left my contact information in hopes of speaking with someone to get an idea of pricing.

On Monday morning, I was delivering one of my "Monday Morning Kickstarter" meetings with a sales team for a client when my cell phone rang. I glanced over at the unrecognizable number and ignored the call. Later in the day, I received an email from the awning company referencing the earlier call and suggesting I book a meeting to speak with them about an awning.

I took a moment to reply to the email, asking for an idea of the budget range for the size of the awning I was considering. If the awning was within our budget, we could have a call. I didn't receive a response, but I did receive a reply that suggested I book a meeting to discuss my question with someone in the company.

On Tuesday, around the same time (9:17 am, to be exact), my phone rang again. This time, I recognized the number (it was the salesperson at the awning company) and let it go to voicemail. Later that day, I received an email again. However, it didn't acknowledge or respond to my question from the previous day; instead, it suggested that I should book a meeting again.

On Wednesday, I received no call, just an email once again asking me to book a meeting. Then, on Friday, I received another email stating, "This will be the last time we reach out to you."

There is a lot wrong with this approach to me as a potential lead, from the lack of response to my question to the "this will be my last email." However, if you charted the follow-up on behalf of the sales professional, it would be a slow decline in outreach over the week or a deceleration. In other words, they started with several points of contact and slowly reduced these contact points as the week progressed. From my experience, this is how many sales professionals pursue leads. They obtain a prospect's name and contact information and then go after that person with a vengeance, only to slowly back off their efforts as time progresses, and they receive no response. For example, they start by reaching out with several emails, calls, or DMs; however, as time progresses, and they hear nothing back, they begin to reduce their outreach; eventually, presuming "no response = no interest," they give up.

Unfortunately, this approach does little to earn attention and pique interest in connecting with you and, in some situations, works in the favor of your prospect. For example, there are likely several messages in your inbox or LinkedIn messages where someone has reached out several times only to stop. Some even tell you, "This is the last time I'll attempt to reach you," as if they are willing you to drop everything and ask for a meeting!

Your goal must be to slowly build awareness, no different from building a relationship with someone you are dating. You wouldn't hit them with four DMs or emails in one day because you don't want to look desperate.

Well, the same philosophy applies here. You aim to ease your way into their world and become a trusted advisor in your expertise. As author and direct marketing strategist Dan Kennedy[3] likes to say, your goal is to become a welcome guest, not an annoying pest.

Hitting anyone with a glut of calls and emails, only to disappear into the abyss within a week or two, is NOT the pathway to becoming a welcome guest. What's the alternative? Well, for starters, try accelerating your outreach. Ease your way into the world of your prospect and allow them to get to know you (and the value you can provide) over a more extended period. Additionally, start slowly, reducing the time between outreach as you progress. The objective here is to build urgency, and various studies have found this effective in getting a response from your prospect.

Here is an example of what that might look like:

Day 1 = Outreach #1
Day 8 = Outreach #2
Day 14 = Outreach #3
Day 20 = Outreach #4
Day 25 = Outreach #5
Day 29 = Outreach #6
Day 30 = Outreach #7
Day 31 = Outreach #8

If you haven't made contact or received a response after following this sequence, start again from the top.

Of course, this approach also presumes you are reaching out in ways and with messages that are prospect-centric, filled with value, and provocative enough to capture attention.

3.2 PLANTING SEEDS OF VALUE

You wouldn't go fishing without bait, so why would you ever connect with a prospect without offering something they perceive as valuable? You may not be as familiar with value-based selling as you are with the idea of using value to earn the undivided attention of your prospect. I call this using value assets, the seeds you'll plant as you attempt to earn the attention of and engage with your prospects.

In terms of prospecting, let's first define what value is and what it isn't.

Value is anything you develop, share, or provide that assists your prospect in better understanding, assessing, and navigating their decision to purchase your product or service. Value can be tangible (e.g., a self-assessment) or intangible (e.g., your responsiveness to your prospects' questions).

Examples of what represents value can vary widely, depending on what you sell, but are typically something easily sharable and understood by your prospect that differentiates you from your competition.

Additionally, the value should be something that enables your prospect to recognize how your product or service would be beneficial (to them) and assists them in navigating their buying decision.

Let's look at some examples of tangible assets broken down by industry.

Value for Selling Insurance:

- Self-diagnosis for Assessing Insurance Coverage
- Template Demonstrating Insurance Investment Options
- White Paper Discussing the Risks of Over-Insuring

Value for Selling Financial Services:

- Booklet Filled with (relevant) Client Testimonials
- White Paper Discussing 5 (little-known) Tax Reduction Strategies
- Manifesto on Top Financial Service Misnomers

Value for Selling Capital Equipment:

- Video Showing the Unique Features of the Equipment
- Tour of an Existing (long-term) Customer's Use of (your) Equipment
- Statistics on Equipment Longevity (where your equipment outlasts the competition)

Value for Selling SaaS:

- Demonstrator Video of How Your Software Differentiates from the Competition
- Free Trial Period of Your Software
- Video Testimonials from Satisfied Clients

Here is what I want you to notice about these value assets. I never mentioned providing a marketing brochure, sharing a LinkedIn post or newsletter, or sending a link to your website. Why? Because that's what your competition is likely sending as value, and frankly, it is boring and in no way beneficial to your prospect. They can find these things on their own.

When you recognize that you need value assets to prospect effectively, the obvious question becomes, where can I get more? As a starting point, you can always ask your existing clients and even your prospects the following question: *What information, tools, or resources could I provide you that would help (or would have helped) make a decision related to purchasing our product or service?* or *When you searched for our product or service, what information or resources would have been helpful to identify the best option for you/your company?*

Your value assets should come in various formats, from videos to PDFs, tangible samples to checklists. The goal is to create assets that will be beneficial in supporting your prospect's decision-making while also addressing the fact that your prospects all have different preferences for how they consume information. Referring to studies conducted by Walter Burke Barbe and his colleagues in the 1970s,[4] we know that every individual has three predominant learning styles: visual, auditory, and kinesthetic. In other words, we all have a preferred means to consume and therefore learn from information. For example, I'm a visual learner, so watching a video of someone doing something on YouTube results in a more precise understanding. Alternatively, if you sent me a podcast (auditory) to listen to the same information, I wouldn't have as much of a desire to consume it, and if I did, it wouldn't have the same impact.

My point is that each of your prospects has a preferred learning modality, and we have no way of knowing what their preference is, at least not until we've had a chance to meet in person. To ensure that the value we share gets consumed and is deemed useful, we need to develop it in multiple formats.

Here are some examples of value in different formats:

- **Visual:** Send an explainer video that demonstrates how your product works
- **Visual and Audible:** Share a client testimonial in written or video form
- **Visual and Kinesthetic:** Share a printed checklist on cardstock and mail it to your prospect
- **Visual and Kinesthetic:** Courier a sample of your product to your prospect
- **Visual and Audible:** Share a recorded interview with an existing client

The more you can vary the format of your value assets, the better chance you'll have of ensuring it lands with the impact you seek and ultimately ensures you earn the attention and interest of your prospect.

In addition to developing value assets in various modalities, you'll also need to organize your assets to ensure they provide ever-increasing value relevant to your prospect. For example, when you first send value, it should be designed to share insights with your prospects that gain their attention. As you continue to share value, you'll want to slowly introduce yourself, your company, the benefits of working with you, etc. Diagram 3.1 demonstrates the continued value escalation necessary to ensure your assets land with impact.

Prospect Value Escalation

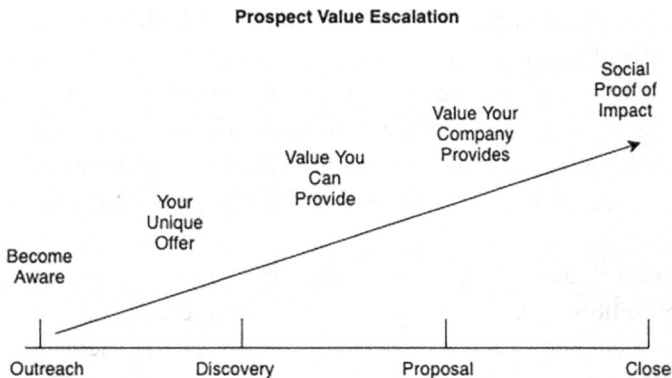

DIAGRAM 3.1
Prospect Value Escalation.

As a starting point, use a simple four-by-four matrix to organize and ensure that sharing value isn't something you have to stop, think about, and develop for every touchpoint for your prospect. That's too much work and will slow down your momentum.

Take ten minutes now, and let's identify your value assets.

3.3 SHAWN'S FIVE STEPS TO DEVELOPING YOUR VALUE ASSETS

1 What questions does your prospect have about your product or service related to their business (remember, you can always ask existing customers or prospects)?
2 What resources, information, samples, demonstrations, testimonials, case studies, etc., can you develop to answer these questions?
3 How can you ensure the information shared is unique or different from what your competitors might share? What's your unique perspective or positioning?
4 What are the various formats in which you can present this value (i.e., audible, visual, and kinesthetic)?
5 Who can you test these assets on to get their feedback on their relevance, impact, and usefulness?

Use a simple 4 × 4 matrix, like Diagram 3.2, to organize your value best.

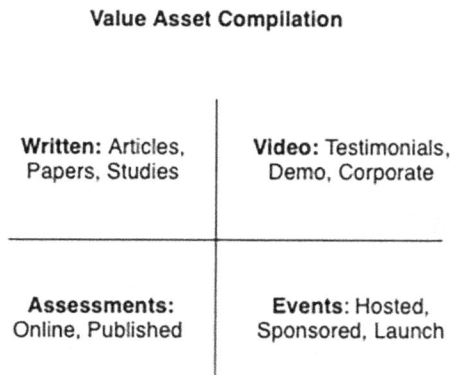

Value Asset Compilation

Written: Articles, Papers, Studies	**Video:** Testimonials, Demo, Corporate
Assessments: Online, Published	**Events:** Hosted, Sponsored, Launch

DIAGRAM 3.2
Value Asset Options.

With your value assets in place, let's discuss how to use them to personalize each prospect's journey and why personalization is key to prospecting success.

3.4 PERSONALIZE EVERY PROSPECT'S JOURNEY

According to a study by Salesforce, 65% of customers expect companies to adapt to their changing needs/preferences.[5] In other words, most (if not all) of your prospects expect you to understand their industry, their company, themselves, and the unique challenges they face. They expect you to know them and provide a personalized experience.

Since we all receive irrelevant cold emails and messages occasionally (or daily!), you know what not to do. For example, in the last week, I've received a request to speak (for free) at a women's conference where everyone else speaking and in attendance is a woman, a request to represent a company that manufactures lighting in Asia, and multiple suggestions on how to improve my YouTube channel subscriber base.

My point is that we all receive impersonal and irrelevant cold inquiries. What you might not realize is that you are inadvertently having this same impact on your cold prospects.

When it comes to personalizing your outreach to prospects, if your immediate thought is, "But Shawn, I include my prospect's first name in all of their emails or direct messages," then you're missing the point. Personalization means that your messaging, questions, positioning, and value assets are all aligned with your prospect's unique and individual needs.

This might seem like a lot of work, and it can be. However, if you don't develop a customized journey for each prospect, you risk being seen as someone who is simply pitching ideas and pushing products, which is highly unlikely to lead to earning attention or engaging at all.

Fortunately, there is a way to create a personalized journey while minimizing the time and energy you need to invest in each prospect. It's a simple resource I developed years ago for the sales teams I train, and I call it the "Prospect Power Planner." It comprises a single sheet of paper and captures all the key elements necessary to provide every prospect with a personalized journey.

3.5 YOUR PROSPECT POWER PLANNER

The Prospect Power Planner consists of various sections designed to capture the most important aspects of each prospect. It enables you to have everything you need in a single document to personalize your prospect's journey.

Get your copy of the Prospect Power Planner at www.unstoppablesalesprospecting.com

Here are the main sections of the planner:

Section 1: Company Background

- What are the core products or services the company sells?
- How many years have they been in business?
- What is their annual revenue?

Section 2: Decision-Makers and Decision-Influencers

- Who is the primary decision-maker (and what is their contact information)?
- Who are the decision-influencers (and what is their contact information)?
- Who are potential referral sources (to reach the decision-maker and/or decision-influencers)?

Section 3: Competition and Key Differentiators (from the competition)

- Who are they buying from today?
- Who else might be attempting to get their business (your competitors)?
- What key differentiators set your products or services apart from these competitors?

Section 4: Provocative Statements and Questions

- What provocative statements will interrupt their patterns?
- What provocative questions will get them thinking differently about your products/services?
- What follow-up questions or statements will allow you to uncover their objectives?

Section 5: Ideal Products or Services (that align with the above)

- What products or services would be best suited for the prospect's application?
- What benefits, outcomes, and improved results will prospects achieve from your products/services?
- What upsell or cross-sell products or services would complement these products?

Section 6: Next Steps and Meeting Time(s)

- What are the logical next steps after your initial meeting?
- When will you meet next (confirmed during the meeting)?

I'll be the first to admit that using the Prospect Power Planner in paper format might seem old-school, and it is for good reason. Studies have repeatedly found that when we write information down (or type it out), our ability to retain that information increases.[6] You can still complete the planner digitally if that's your preference, but there is a reason why doing so with paper and pen is more effective.

Speaking of effectiveness, let me reiterate that the goal of the planner is threefold:

1 Capture the information necessary to create a personalized prospect journey.
2 Have the questions and provocative statements ready to use during the prospect dialogue.
3 Have a resource to follow during the meeting to ensure you stay on plan and capture the next steps, actions, and your next meeting.

In other words, take the planner with you (or open it on your laptop) during your prospect meetings. Let your prospect know you are taking notes from the discussion, and don't worry if you need to take a moment to do so.

Taking this step alone can reinforce your personalization of your prospects' journey and highlight to them just how important they are.

Next, let's dive into building your foundation for more effective prospecting.

UNSTOPPABLE SALES PROSPECTING SYSTEM ACTION STEP

Visit www.unstoppablesalesprospecting.com to download your Prospect Power Planner and complete the exercises listed above. Leave yourself room to add additional notes and ideas as you continue to build your prospecting system.

Part Two

Build Your B2B Prospecting Foundation

When it comes to prospecting, one of the most shocking changes in prospect behavior must be the shift in time allotted to sales. For example, 25 years ago, it was not uncommon for prospects to set aside hours in their weekly calendar to meet with or speak with new sales representatives. In most instances, this didn't include the additional time they'd set aside weekly to connect with sales representatives of the companies they were buying from to address questions and ask about other products or services. They were so willing to commit this time because it was their primary method of staying on top of changes and improvements in products and services.

The evolution of the Internet, AI, and technology in general has negated the need to meet with sales, or at least that's the perception by many prospects. A study from Gartner released only a few years ago identified that 45% of a B2B prospect's "buying time" is dedicated to research, 22% of which is online, and the balance being from offline sources (i.e., events, discussions with peers).[7] The study further explained that prospects were only dedicating 17% of this buying time to meet with sales. Furthermore, the study revealed

DOI: 10.4324/9781003604457-5

that 17% of time spent deciding who to buy from is divided between the number of suppliers or vendors they spoke with. So if your prospect were considering three suppliers, invariably, each salesperson would get approximately 5.33% of the prospect's time when buying that product or service.

There are two critical takeaways from this study. First, many prospects focus on research before engaging with sales. Second, the amount of time a prospect dedicates to meeting and speaking with salespeople is diminishing. As sales professionals, we are increasingly dealing with prospects who believe that they don't need sales in the early stages of a buying decision and can instead learn everything they need from conducting their online and offline research. As you might expect, the outcome of these behaviors is that prospects form opinions on what they read, hear, and observe and look to sales to either complement or disprove their assumptions.

Fortunately, there are strategies to overcome these preconceived notions and assumptions, but they require us to think, act, and behave entirely differently than we may be accustomed to during the prospecting process.

4

Cold Calling Isn't Dead, It's Just Different

The last chapter discussed why your cold outreach isn't working. I shared those reasons so early in the book because setting the tone for what we're about to discuss is essential. There are a growing number of studies, like the one I just shared, that repeatedly show that today's prospects are giving us less time as sales professionals. For example, in the study I shared a moment ago, today's B2B prospects are spending more time researching online and offline as part of the buying process. In turn, this reduces their time spent on sales.[8] Additionally, another Gartner study found that at least 33% of B2B buyers today want a (sales) rep-free experience entirely.[9] Let that sink in for a moment.

Before you drop this book in a panic, let's share some additional points that put these studies into perspective. First, these statistics will vary depending on what you sell and to whom. For example, if you sell SaaS products, insurance, or financial services, you'll likely find that the percentage of prospects who prefer a sales rep-free experience is significantly higher than if you sell capital equipment, manufactured products, or consulting services.

Three factors are driving this variation in B2B prospect behaviors, namely:

Shifting Demographics: Older prospects accustomed to interacting with sales professionals are more inclined to want to continue these interactions. Younger prospects, those who have grown up with and are more technologically savvy, tend to want to use more digital means to research and facilitate their buy.

Advancing Technology: The continued advancement of technology is influencing how buyers buy. AI, for example, diminishes the time it

DOI: 10.4324/9781003604457-6

takes to research and compare solutions online and, as a result, is making it even easier for buyers to perform their research. Additionally, with increasing social platforms advancing their advertising options, prospects are finding products or services in new places, prompting them to become accustomed to making digital purchases for products or services they once would never have considered completing online. For example, as of this writing, you can buy mini excavators on Temu, find and purchase office supplies on TikTok, and invest in specific consulting services while scrolling on YouTube.

Misdirected Sales Methods: Many sales professionals today use sales practices that they have been told (often through outdated or ineffective sales training) are productive or efficient, yet only serve to turn buyers off. For example, many sales representatives still send cold emails, focused primarily on introducing themselves and discussing their products and their company, which are completely irrelevant and useless when it comes to earning the attention of their prospects. They use an automated dialer to call dozens of prospects simultaneously and then fail to engage the prospect quickly when (and if) the prospect answers the phone. They invest hours of their time each week scrolling LinkedIn, liking various posts of their prospects, mistakenly believing that this will somehow lead to a sale. Although you might think (or be told) these are effective, they do nothing more than irritate prospects.

In this book, our goal is to become unstoppable in our prospecting and set ourselves apart from our competition. We will differentiate our approach, methods, and language to earn attention and engage in a dialogue. So, our starting point is to address the age-old premise that cold calling is dead. It isn't, but it's likely not what you think it is.

4.1 THE EVOLUTION OF A COLD CALL

When I sold cars back in the early 2000s, the telephone (we're talking old-school, 12-button, coiled corded phones) was a tool we used as part of the sales process. The reason? Email was in its infancy, meaning that although I had an email address and could send and receive emails, not everyone was using email as a common communication method. There was also no social media and very little happening online in the way of websites.

The telephone was a tool we used to try to reach a prospect and convince them to come to or return to the dealership. As an example of how we used the phone, it was common on rainy days to "work the phones," making outbound calls to reconnect with past and prospective customers. If you stopped by, for example, and we had a conversation, test-drove a vehicle, or discussed purchasing a car, the phone was the primary method to reach out and follow up with you or re-engage you to return to the dealership.

The telephone was effective because everyone had one and was accustomed to using one. There was no "call display," and since everyone used a telephone to communicate with family and friends, the chances that a prospect would answer your call were extremely high.

If we contrast this against how most people use the telephone today, we see a very different picture. On the positive side, nearly everyone has a phone today (even more so than in years past), and they carry that phone with them almost all the time. However, the way we use phones has changed. It's no longer a primary communication tool but a tertiary means of communication. In other words, most people don't default to "call-first"; instead, they arrange a call after communicating on other primary communication channels. You could send information via email to a prospect and then suggest a call to discuss. Since the phone is no longer a primary communication channel for most people, especially in business, we need to consider how it is integrated into communication today, which informs how best to use the phone as part of our prospecting process.

There are three considerations for you to make when it comes to assessing if you'll include the telephone as part of your prospecting process, as follows:

1. **Prospect Demographics**: Older prospects, those over 50, are more inclined to answer the phone, considering they've used it as a primary communication channel. If you are prospecting individuals you know are over 50, the phone should still be a step in your prospecting process. You might not lead with it, but it should be a step you move to if your other communication methods fall flat.
2. **Reliance on Email**: If your prospecting process requires you to use email as part of your outreach and/or follow-up, the greatest obstacle you have today is that, increasingly, companies are ratcheting up their spam folders. More than likely, your emails will land in a spam folder

at some point and will not be seen by your prospect. The phone can be a great way to ensure your emails aren't landing in a spam folder, as you can call and leave a message that points someone to your email. For example, "Hello Bob, it's Shawn calling. I sent you a quick email earlier this week, but I'm not sure if it landed in your inbox . . ." (Author's Note: We'll get more into calling and email scripts later in the book).

3. **Portability**: If your prospects don't spend much time at their desk, the phone can be the best way to reach them. Most of your prospects you sell to, particularly those who don't see a lot of desk time, carry their phone with them. In many instances, this might be 24/7, 365. Earlier in my career, I managed a company but traveled a lot. My phone was something I used regularly, from checking messages and emails to making calls. Roles that don't see much desk time tend to avoid using online meetings like Zoom or Teams, as they cannot easily participate. These roles include production managers who walk the production floor most of the day, busy CEOs, and executives who travel regularly. With these roles, prospects are more likely to answer a call because it is one of the few ways to reach them, and as a result, they are more accustomed to and comfortable picking up a call.

As you will note above, you have fewer chances today to connect with prospects via the telephone. For those who do answer, there's a greater likelihood they will be comfortable hanging up on you if they don't know you or deem you or your message to be relevant.

4.2 COLD CALLING AS YOUR DIFFERENTIATOR

If you are not using cold calling today, or you're inclined to skip this section because cold calling isn't something you believe is relevant, considering what you sell, I'd encourage you to reconsider. Although cold calling might seem archaic or ineffective with some prospects (i.e., you are attempting to reach a young, desk-bound manager or executive who spends most of their time using email and direct messaging as their primary communication methods), this may be why you should use the phone.

You need to consider your competitor's prospecting when it comes to your chosen prospecting methods. Your competitors are likely practicing the same methods of prospecting that you are, which is not a good thing. For example, if your competitors rely on sending messages using specific communication channels (e.g., email, LinkedIn), then the phone may be a way for you to stand out among your competitors, and that's a good thing.

When I speak at sales kickoff meetings or association events, I often use the catchphrase *"Same Doesn't Sell"* to raise awareness that to earn the attention of your prospect, you must set yourself apart from your competitor in every way possible. Differentiation is critical, so if no one else uses the phone as part of their outreach, you should!

You can incorporate the phone as part of your prospecting process and differentiate yourself in different ways. If you think that cold calling is outdated or that using it as a differentiator may backfire and hurt your prospect's first impressions, think again. According to Zippia, an average of 49% of buyers prefer initial contact be made via cold call.[10] A study by RAIN Group suggested that this percentage increases to 57% for C-level executives and VPs who prefer cold calling as the preferred method of being contacted.[11]

The question then isn't whether you should include cold calling but how to use it to earn attention and accelerate trust with your prospect. Let's look at some best practices to ensure your cold calling effectively earns attention and trust. These are a compilation of publicly available statistics and best practices based on work with my clients, all designed to provide you with a guideline for using the phone to prospect.

4.3 COLD CALLING BEST PRACTICES (STATISTICS)

- Make cold calls between 4:00 pm and 5:00 pm, followed by 11:00 am and 12:00 pm. (Outplay).[12]
- Wednesdays and Thursdays are considered the best days to make cold calls (Gong.com).[13]
- Call the prospect by their first name, and then transition to a simple greeting that suggests previous contact. Gong.io did a study and found that using "How have you been?" performed 6X better than any other opening phrase.[13]
- After your opening, explain the reason for your call. By transitioning quickly to explain why you are calling, you'll keep your prospect on the phone longer, allowing you to engage them in a discussion.[13]

- If you have difficulty reaching a prospect via the phone, try calling them on a Friday afternoon between 3 pm and 5 pm. Most people have fewer meetings on Friday afternoons, and an increasing number of companies ban Friday meetings.[14]

4.4 COLD CALLING STEPS

To prepare to cold call your prospects, follow the steps below:

1. **Research**: Set time aside weekly, typically on Mondays and Tuesdays, to complete your pre-call research.
2. **Scripts**: Develop written scripts to guide your outreach, including your greeting, which should incorporate the points shared in the best practices above. You should have different scripts for different kinds of prospects (i.e., each prospect persona should have its own scripts to align with individual priorities and needs).
3. **Calls**: Block time in your calendar to make your calls, considering the best practices listed above. The amount of time you set aside will be dependent on your role. For example, someone in business development might set 20+ hours aside for outbound calls. In contrast, a sales agent who manages their existing customers and prospects for new ones might set aside one hour per day. Treat this time as if it were a meeting with a prospect – no cancellations or delays.
4. **Targets**: Although statistics for each industry are different, your outreach calls (to pursue outbound sales) should range between 100 and 200 calls per week.
5. **Follow-Ups**: Your initial calls will require follow-up. This can include additional calls or using other communication forms, such as email. You should plan for at least eight follow-ups and, therefore, need to block time in your calendar to make this happen. For phone follow-ups, refer to the best practices listed above.
6. **Tools**: You may choose to use an autodialer such as Dialpad or Kixie to support your outbound calling efforts. Some autodialers offer the ability to record calls (to assess your performance), whereas others do not. Some software includes AI that can support automated dialing.

Cold Calling Framework

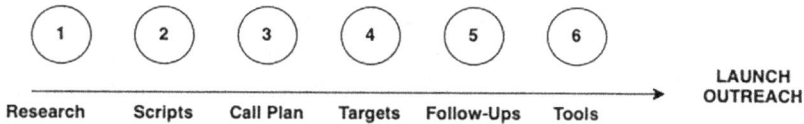

DIAGRAM 4.1
Cold Calling Framework.

Diagram 4.1 provides an overview of your Cold Calling Steps. You can also get a copy of your Cold Call Worksheet at www.unstoppablesalesprospecting.com.

With these steps in place for cold calling, let's dive into some best practices to improve you further.

4.5 MODERNIZING THE COLD CALL

At this point in the book, I'm presuming you fall into one of three categories of readers. First, cold calling is part of your prospecting process, and you're looking for some tips and strategies to increase its effectiveness. Alternatively, you aren't using cold calling, but you have decided that your prospects meet the criteria above, and you'd like to incorporate cold calling as part of your prospecting process. Or, in the case of the third group, you've decided cold calling will not be effective for your prospects, in which case I'd encourage you to test some of the steps we've discussed to be sure. You'll be surprised who cold calling will work with.

Considering we've already provided some best practices to elevate your cold calling success, let's take a few minutes to share some additional insights to make your cold calling as effective as possible.

According to Zoominfo,[15] cold calling results in the following:

- 80% of unrecognized calls go directly to voicemail
- Recipients don't return 90% of first-time voicemails
- The average voicemail response is 4.8%

Although these statistics may seem gloomy, let's examine them to understand how cold calling can support more effective prospecting.

Cold Calling Insight #1: Unrecognized calls go directly to voicemail.

Since most unrecognized calls go directly to voicemail, we can capitalize on this to warm up your prospect. In other words, it's likely your competitors aren't bothering with calling, considering it antiquated or outdated. This offers us an opportunity to incorporate a cold call as part of our outreach process, which then becomes unique and helps us stand out in the minds of our prospects.

Further, since nearly every prospect carries a phone with them, and cell phone numbers are increasingly being shared as primary numbers, we are confident we are reaching the prospect directly (you can't always say this when you send a cold email, which increasingly lands in spam folders). So, by making a call, even if it goes to voicemail, you know you are making direct contact with your prospect—and if they pick up their phone, even better!

Cold Calling Insight #2: Recipients don't return 90% of first-time voice messages.

The goal of your voice message should be to highlight earlier or other forms of communication that you have or intend to share. In other words, mention that you sent an email, a package, or a LinkedIn message. Since the statistics suggest you're unlikely to get a callback, use voicemail to draw their attention to other, more robust messages you've sent. Doing so provides a pathway past spam filters, where an email or message from you might be waiting. You can call and leave a message before you send an email, for example, "Hi Julie, I was going to send you a quick email . . ." or after you send an email, "Tom, it's Shawn calling, and I wanted to confirm my email make its way to you. . . ."

Although your prospect might not return your call, there is a 100% chance they will listen to at least a part of your voice message (if they don't, their voicemail box will fill up and be unusable). By leaving a voice message, you can ensure that your message (which should include an energetic greeting and the reason for your call) will be received. This supports creating further awareness and earning your prospects' attention.

Cold Calling Insight #3: The average voicemail response is 4.8%.

One final point on using cold calls as part of your prospecting outreach is that there is a slight chance that your prospect will contact you after hearing your voice message, so always provide options to connect with you. For example, the end of your message might say, "I'll follow up via email; however, feel free to contact me via phone or text at 514-555-1212."

Let me reinforce this point by suggesting that every contact point you have with a prospect should always include clear options for how to reach you. Can you imagine someone listening to your message and then thinking, "Okay, I have a few minutes, let me call them back . . . wait, I don't have a number?" To say this would be tragic is an understatement.

Despite your initial presumptions about using cold calling as part of your prospecting, I hope I've convinced you that it can be a vital differentiator for your prospecting system. Before we wrap up this chapter, I have one final point to share with you that's of utmost importance. The same stats I provided from ZoomInfo also found that a well-crafted voicemail can improve response rates from 3% to 22%. In other words, the more effort you put into designing and implementing a well-crafted call script, the better your chances of getting attention and response are. Here is a simple overview of the core components of your cold calling script.

Components of a Cold Call Script:

1 A brief greeting
2 Your name
3 A compelling reason for your call
4 Your next step
5 An easy way to contact you

Here is an example: "Hi John, it's Shawn calling from ABC Insurance. I wanted to reach out on Joe Smith's recommendation from your Northeastern Division. He suggested we should speak. I'll send a brief email this afternoon with further information; however, feel free to call or text me back at 514-555-1212. I look forward to speaking."

Despite many of today's sales strategies focusing on low-touch, high-tech prospecting to introduce more technology to automate the process, consider that cold calling can be a primary method for you to build awareness and earn attention.

Now it's your turn. Visit www.unstoppablesalesprospecting.com to get your cold call template and map your script and its placement in your prospecting outreach.

In the next chapter, we'll discuss strategies to improve your email as part of your prospecting process!

UNSTOPPABLE SALES PROSPECTING SYSTEM ACTION STEP

How might you incorporate making calls or leaving messages into your prospecting system? What are the likely benefits of doing so? What are some example scripts you can prepare and test to determine their impact on convincing prospects to call you back or look for your email?

5

Email Has a Purpose (And It's Not What You Think)

It's rare to find a sales professional who doesn't use email as a tool in their prospecting. Despite the increasing lack of response, particularly when sending cold emails, email is one of the most effective ways to reach a cold prospect. According to a study by RAIN Group, 80% of buyers prefer to be contacted by email.[16] Interestingly, this study also references that more buyers prefer to be contacted by email than those who use email for their cold outreach, which is 78% of sales professionals.

Since we know emails are an effective and acceptable way to connect with cold prospects, how can we increase their effectiveness to improve and receive more positive and timely responses? The answer to this question isn't simple and borders on some psychology that's at play in many instances; however, in this chapter, we'll dive in to provide you with the steps, methods, and framework to amplify the success of your cold email prospecting.

5.1 SENDING EMAILS THAT GET OPENED REQUIRES SKILL

When I started speaking professionally in 2009, the first few talks I delivered were mediocre. I used a lot of slides that were heavy in text and spent a lot of my time hanging close to the podium to read notes or, worse yet, reading directly from the slides. Looking back at one of the early videos that captured my first keynote, it is painful to watch. Fortunately, things have changed (according to the feedback I regularly receive at sales kickoff meetings and

DOI: 10.4324/9781003604457-7

association events). If you've seen me speak, you'll know that I don't use notes; I walk the stage or floor to interact with audience members, including relevant humor, and if I do use slides, they contain mostly images. It's a stark contrast from those early days.

Reaching this skill level as a professional speaker took 15 years. I continue to add to those skills daily as I observe and apply different methods and strategies to improve my craft and create a more powerful experience for each audience. I share this with you for a reason. Getting good at anything requires learning the skill and practicing, applying, and repeating. Not surprising, I realize, but then let me ask you, if this is the case with any skill, why don't most sales professionals invest their time, effort, and money into learning how to use email for prospecting? All you need to do is open your spam folder, and you'll likely find dozens (if not hundreds) of lengthy, self-focused, boring emails sent by someone who sells. Worse yet, when you receive one of these pointless emails, what first impression does it create about the individual, their company, product, or service? Most likely, the sender is lazy, annoying, and overly focused on their needs (to make a sale) versus yours.

Let me share an example. A few years ago, I was considering building a garage, so I visited various websites. The following is a cold email I received (some of the information has been changed to protect the sender) from someone trying to sell me a prefabricated garage after I visited their website and left a question in the contact form to ask about their options for a 20′ × 30′ building.

– Example Email:

Subject: ABC Buildings Is Your Building of Choice
Dear Mr. Casemore,

It's my pleasure to introduce myself. My name is Don Smith and my company, ABC Buildings, is in the great city of Walla Walla, Washington. We are a family-owned business and believe that every customer deserves to receive the exact building that they want. We pride ourselves on providing options that satisfy every customer's building needs.

We have been manufacturing high-quality prefabricated buildings since 1987. Our wide range of building sizes, layouts, and finishes allows our customers to select a prefab building that best suits their needs. We are ISO-certified, which gives our customers confidence that every building we manufacture is of the highest quality.

Our building sizes range from 6′ × 8′ to 60′ × -40′, with or without lofts. Depending on your application, we offer ceiling heights of 10′, 12′, and 16′.

All our models include customized window and door sizes and can come from our factory with a fully finished interior. Some examples of our interior finish options include:

- Insulated with R20 insulation
- R20 spray foam insulation
- Drywall, paneling, or plastic interior walls and ceilings
- Electrical and water outlets

I would like to arrange a call with you to share some examples of our prefab buildings and learn more about your building needs. Please use this link to arrange a meeting with me at your convenience to discuss how we can meet your building needs.

Looking forward to hearing back from you.

Regards,

Don Smith

– End

I share this email with you because it demonstrates what you should not do when cold emailing a prospect. Don has structured this overly formal email as a general response or outreach to his prospects. There are many, many problems with his email, but let's start with the most obvious.

- It's overly formal and isn't personalized to me
- It's focused on the seller and what's of importance to them
- It's too lengthy and overly verbose
- It puts the onus on me to do something (i.e., please arrange a call)

When sending your prospects a cold email, here's what you need to recognize. An effective cold email will earn your prospect's attention if it compels them to act. In other words, structure your emails to entice the reader to open, read, and respond. Numerous studies have been conducted on creating compelling emails, so below, I've captured what I've found to be the most important aspects to consider incorporating into your emails.

Over the years, I've invested in various email marketing certifications. Although I may not be a marketing guru, these programs helped provide insights on the best structure and format of emails to earn attention. I suggest that you do the same. You can check out HubSpot for free email marketing programs to help you develop your email skills.

Warning! If you do start to dig into this topic online, you'll find a wide array of so-called experts providing you with examples of templates to use. Many of these require investing in their programs, so be careful who you listen to. Below is a template to get you started.

Here are some statistics and best practices I've compiled based on my experiences working with sales professionals and sales teams globally. Let's begin with a few important considerations you should make when attempting to structure an email that gets read by your prospect, for example:

- You have 51 seconds to earn a reader's interest[17]
- Most readers scan their emails using an F pattern, starting with the opening line, skimming the following line or two, and then moving down vertically
- Emails that end with a call to action (or CTA) guide readers to take the next step[18]
- People respond to your email when you trigger a response in their brain by incorporating curiosity, reciprocity, social proof, and scarcity[19]

Considering these factors, here are some considerations for crafting a compelling email that gets your prospects to read and respond.

5.2 ESSENTIAL ELEMENTS OF YOUR COLD EMAIL

1. A strong subject line:
   - Keep it brief, between four and seven words
   - Avoid exclamation or spam words (Urgent, Act Now, etc.)
   - Contain an action word (i.e., Reduce, Increase, Improve)
2. A personalized greeting:
   - Avoid being too formal (i.e., Good Day Sir)
   - Avoid being overly personalized (i.e., Hey Sara)

3. A relevant and compelling opening line
   - Why did you contact them (i.e., referred, drove past their office, etc.)?
   - Relevant statistics or data impacting their business (i.e., "A recent report . . .")
   - Likely impact or consequences to their business or division (validated by market)
4. Introduction of you, your company, how you address the impacts, and social proof
   - Your name and your company name
   - A statement about how you help companies address the impacts described
   - Examples of (relevant) companies you've assisted with these impacts
5. A call to action
   - What would you suggest is the next step?
   - Keep this as simple as possible
6. Personalized sign-off
   - Avoid being overly formal (i.e., "Thank you, sir.")
   - Avoid being overly informal (i.e., "Check-ya Later")

The length of your email using the above framework should consist of five to six sentences at the most with one sentence for each section. Additionally, you should put space between each sentence to create separation in the content so it stands out. Let's use this framework to recreate Don Smith's email from earlier so you can see the difference.
– Example Email

> Subject: Prefabricated 20′ × 30′ Buildings
> Hello Shawn,
> Thank you for submitting your question about our 20′ × 30′ buildings.
>
> From your address, snow load is something you're likely considering. A recent study by Building Study North America found our frames to be the strongest in the industry, able to withstand extreme snow loads.
>
> My name is Don Smith. ABC Buildings has been building and supplying high-strength, high-quality, and fully customizable prefabricated buildings since 1972. Our buildings have won numerous awards

for withstanding natural disasters and anything Mother Nature can throw at them.

Would it make sense to arrange a brief call to clarify a few things so I can make some recommendations?

Looking forward to speaking.

Regards,

Don Smith

– End

Do you notice the difference? The first email is all about Don and his company. This second email is about me and my needs, briefly mentioning how Don (and his company) can help. You'll also notice this email is significantly shorter than the original.

To clarify, whether your prospect sent in an inquiry is irrelevant. If Don stumbled across me posting on Facebook about my needs in a relevant group, he could send this same email structure with only an adjustment to the first sentence.

You'll also notice that Don demonstrated that he understood my needs based on where I lived, making his email all the more relevant. In other words, Don would have researched to ensure this email lands nicely. Sure, research takes time, but would you rather pursue a small number of highly targeted prospects with relevant messages or send hundreds or even thousands of irrelevant emails in hopes they land (and likely get labeled a spammer in the process)? I prefer the former because the chances of getting to the call (which is the next step in this example) are far higher.

With this structure in place, let's discuss some common mistakes that sales professionals have made when sending cold emails and how you can avoid them.

5.3 MISTAKES TO AVOID WHEN EMAILING PROSPECTS

If you follow the instructions above, you'll have a significantly better chance of prospects responding to your cold emails. However, there are some mistakes that I see sales professionals repeatedly make when sending emails, most often because they follow their misguided instincts or because of something they've read that is false or misguided.

- **Lengthy Emails**: According to various studies, the ideal length of a cold email that prompts a response is 50–125 words. Remember, your goal from a cold email (or any cold outreach for that matter) is to engage the prospect or get them to respond in the case of an email. When an email is lengthy, even if the reader's initial scan suggests it's worth reading, chances are they will set it aside to read when they have time, which unfortunately will never come because they will forget about it.

- **Impersonal Emails**: You might think this category is about ensuring you include your prospects and company names in your email. Well, that's a good start, but when you consider that a prospect doesn't know you, the tendency is to share information about you, your company, and your products or services. To be truthful, no one cares at this stage. If you were to run into someone at an event in person, would you spend time asking questions to get to know them or spending 15 minutes telling them about you? When you drone on about yourself, your company, or your product, you turn off prospects who want to hear about themselves. Focus your email on what you know of them (from your research) and how you can help them. Later in the conversation, you can get to the other stuff (you, your background, your company, etc.).

- **Lack of Email Relevance**: Focusing your email on you more than the prospect won't get you a response to your cold email. Neither will an irrelevant email. These emails share information that is neither important nor timely to your prospect. For example, if your research suggests most of your prospects are looking to reduce costs, adding a general statement such as "our product can help you reduce costs" isn't relevant; it's vague and too general. Instead, be more specific. Suppose your product reduces your prospect's costs; a more specific (and therefore more relevant) statement might be, "Our other manu-facturing clients have found that our ___ product reduces operating costs by 15–25% in the first 3 months." Do you see the difference? If you know your product or service can help your prospect, be more specific. Doing so ensures relevance and piques curiosity, which can lead to a response.

- **Poor Email Timing**: Numerous studies have been conducted on the best times to send emails to increase your chances of a response. Unfortunately, many studies have conflicting information (i.e., some say to avoid sending emails on Mondays, while others suggest you should send emails on Mondays). Additionally, there are numerous outside factors to consider, such as time zones, email servers, and the varying priorities of your prospects (i.e., how their day is structured).

Here are some basic rules that I've found should be applied most of the time when sending cold emails if the goal is to engage in a discussion and/or get a response, as follows:

1. Send cold emails to arrive in the late morning (i.e., between 10 am and 12 pm) and late afternoon (3 pm and 5 pm) for your prospect.
2. Avoid sending cold emails on Monday mornings.
3. If a prospect responds to you, immediately reply, even if it suggests a different date to speak. For example, if a prospect replies to you on Sunday at 8 pm and you see this email, you should reply.

Author Note: I support pursuing a balanced life, particularly for sales professionals. So, you choose when you respond to or engage with a prospect; however, keep in mind when they reply to you, it is a sign that they have decided that it is the time to invest in you, so if you miss this window, there's a good chance you've missed the opportunity to engage. Your lack of response (i.e., I'll wait until Monday morning) can also send the wrong message about how responsive to be. To be clear, I'm not suggesting you respond to everyone immediately; however, for cold prospects you've been pursuing, you'll want to send the right message to get the relationship off on the right foot.

- **Weak or misleading subject line**: Your subject line opens your email and is the most essential part of your email. When you create subject lines that are overly lengthy or contain potential spam words (e.g., Act Now, Important! Urgent!), you reduce the chances of engagement and increase the chances of your email going to spam. In both instances, prospects will likely never read them.
- **Lack of Transparency**: If you send emails and use other forms of communication, such as leaving voice messages or sending DMs through LinkedIn or other social platforms, you need to be transparent about your efforts. For example, if you are sending a cold

email after attempting to connect through different means, say "Hi Gabriela, I left you a voice message last week but wanted to follow up here," or "Hello Jon, not sure if you saw my LinkedIn message, however, wanted to try and connect here." If you aren't transparent about your other efforts, chances are you'll be deemed a spammer or someone disconnected from your prospect's best interests. Remember, just because your prospect doesn't respond to your message doesn't mean they didn't read it.

- **Misalignment of Communication Styles**: One consideration you'll need to make when using email to reach prospects is always to consider what you are selling and to whom you are selling it. The answer to this question will inform the amount of detail to include in your emails (and other forms of communication, for that matter). For example, selling a highly technical solution, such as customized software, to an analytical person, such as a Director of IT, will require more detail in your outreach. Alternatively, selling parts to a maintenance manager should contain less detail and you should be more direct in your language. Your behaviors and communication preferences should not be part of the equation. For example, if you are a highly analytical person by nature, trying to reach those less so, your inclination is to include a lot of detail in your emails. According to the work of psychologists like William Marston,[20] whom we referenced earlier, your behavior informs your actions. In other words, your desire for additional details leads you to believe the individual receiving your email (or other communication) also wants details. Remember, the goal in cold outreach, using cold emails, is to engage a prospect and get them to respond, not to bore them to tears with an overly lengthy email they have no time (or desire) to reach.

In this chapter, you've identified and avoided common mistakes sales professionals make and have structured a well-thought-out, personalized, effective email. Now suppose that your cold emails begin getting more responses (which they will!), resulting in you connecting with the prospect, having a meaningful discussion either through email or in some other way to speak (i.e., virtual meeting, in-person meeting, telephone, etc.) and then for no apparent reason, the prospect ghosts you. How can you get your prospect to re-engage?

5.4 HOW TO RESPOND IF YOU'VE BEEN GHOSTED

Often, I get asked how to respond and re-engage a prospect if they ghost you. If you aren't sure what ghosting is, it's when a prospect with whom you've engaged disappears into thin air. In other words, you've had some discussions, and then suddenly, without notice or reason, they stop responding to all forms of communication. Being ghosted can be highly frustrating. After all, you've invested significant time in pursuing a prospect and had some meaningful conversations, and suddenly, they stop responding to you.

In my experience, one of the best ways to re-engage a prospect after being ghosted is through email. However, this can be done using written text within an email or a brief video embedded within an email (i.e., software such as Vidyard offers the capability to do this).

The other consideration is the language you should use within your message to entice your prospect to re-engage. If you've done everything right during initial discussions with your prospect, you must appeal to their emotions to draw them out of their silence. In my experience, they've likely ghosted you for one of several reasons, such as:

- They have other, more urgent priorities to deal with
- They've decided to go another direction (i.e., chosen a different supplier or provider)
- Their priorities have been re-prioritized (i.e., different projects to work on)
- The budget they were planning to use has been cut or eliminated
- Their current supplier retained them using an incentive
- They were fired or resigned from their job

Of course, there is a chance that something you said or did during the initial conversations or meetings didn't land well, for whatever reason, leading them to ghost you. For now, however, we'll presume this is not true. To be clear, being ghosted repeatedly suggests there is something that you are saying or doing that is driving your prospects away.

Presuming it's unlikely you did anything wrong, it's essential to draw a parallel between the impact their ghosting has on you personally (i.e., loss of a good prospect, loss of an opportunity) and their reason for ghosting you. When you appeal to their emotions, you can, in turn, influence their willingness to give you a few minutes of their time to explain what has happened or changed.

The structure of the message I would suggest you use to re-engage your prospect is as follows:

1. Greeting
2. Last Left-off + Unfortunate result
3. Personal plea
4. Sign-off

Keep this short and to the point, ensuring they read (or watch) your message and don't see it as something they should review later. Here is an example:

> Dear Julie,
> The last time we spoke, we discussed assessing your commercial insurance needs. Unfortunately, we haven't been able to make this happen.
> Was it something that I did or didn't do?
> Regards,
> Shawn

That's it. Short, sweet, and to the point.

This type of message structure will get you a response at least 40% of the time, although it may not happen immediately. To minimize your chances of being ghosted in the first place, you need to have a prospecting system that includes other forms of communication. So, let's tackle this by incorporating one of the most potent and effective B2B prospecting methods, LinkedIn.

UNSTOPPABLE SALES PROSPECTING SYSTEM ACTION STEP

What improvements should you make to your cold emails? Use the example script provided with your own information to determine what impacts it might have on your response rate. Also, if someone has ghosted you, test the Ghosted Script for yourself!

6

LinkedIn

Your Not-so-Secret Weapon

Regarding B2B prospecting, two factors are essential in determining your success. The first is being clear on your ideal prospects so that you invest your time pursuing those who offer you the most incredible opportunity to make a sale. The second is to spend your time where those ideal prospects spend theirs. Historically, this meant joining the country club where your prospects hang out, becoming a member of the association your prospects belong to, and participating in events your prospects attend. These are all still relevant options; however, considering the studies shared earlier, your prospects spend considerable time researching their purchases online. To state the obvious, as sales professionals, we need to spend time online anywhere they may conduct this research. LinkedIn is one place where you should spend time as a sales professional.

To begin with, if you are unfamiliar with LinkedIn or not convinced it's a place to spend time when it comes to B2B sales, let me share a few statistics that suggest otherwise:

- 4 out of 5 of LinkedIn's 900 million members are decision-makers who drive business decisions[21]
- Salespeople who engage on LinkedIn are 51% more likely to hit their sales quotas than those who don't[22]
- By 2025, 80% of B2B sales interactions will take place digitally[23]

If these statistics don't convince you to spend more time on LinkedIn as part of your prospecting, I'm unsure what will. Before we dive deeply into LinkedIn, however, let me suggest that your profile is one of the most critical pieces of the LinkedIn puzzle. For example, when a prospect finds you

DOI: 10.4324/9781003604457-8

or hears from you on LinkedIn, one of the first things they'll do is check out your profile, so it needs to be complete, relevant, and resourceful. To learn more about improving your profile, check out LinkedIn's Social Selling Index, a free tool to assess the strength of your profile. You can get your free score at https://business.linkedin.com/sales-solutions/social-selling/the-social-selling-index-ssi.

Additionally, if you use LinkedIn, you must be active on the platform, periodically sharing or publishing relevant information for your prospects. Presuming you are and you've built a powerful profile, let's explore how to use LinkedIn as part of your Unstoppable Sales[SM] Prospecting System.

6.1 DON'T PITCH, ENGAGE

Recognizing the power of LinkedIn in finding and connecting with your prospects, let's start by dispelling the myth that simply liking and commenting on your prospect's posts will get you a sale. They won't. Additionally, this kind of activity can be highly time-consuming. For example, suppose you are pursuing 20 prospects and you've determined that by liking or commenting on their posts, you are "warming them up." First, we must presume that your prospect will be within your network, which is not always the case.

Additionally, they will need to accept your connection request, which is not guaranteed. Lastly, keep in mind that your prospects have seen this behavior before. Every day, they see random strangers suddenly appear in their comments; they then receive a connection request, followed by a pitch message if they accept the connection. Essentially, they've seen this approach repeatedly and know what you are trying to achieve. Remember, our goal is to differentiate ourselves from competitors, so we need a better, more effective way to engage.

Aside from the fact this can be ineffective, it can also be a massive waste of time. Suppose you spend 20 minutes per prospect doing this activity each week. That equates to almost 7 hours each week of searching, liking, and commenting. That's a day of your week gone without any real results. There is a better way.

Let's start by returning to my earlier point that the goal of your message, be it through email, LinkedIn, or other channels when you are prospecting, is to get a response. When you think of each step in your prospecting process as a small goal, it not only makes your prospecting more effective, but you will also feel more successful. Simply liking or commenting on someone's post is highly unlikely to get a response other than a possible "thank-you" in the comments section. Let's also be clear that I'm not suggesting you send long-winded, self-centered InMails to your prospects either. The same rules apply to your email: keep them brief, seek a chance to connect, and apply to LinkedIn. So, what is the best way to use LinkedIn to engage with your prospects?

There are five steps to follow when it comes to using LinkedIn for Prospecting, as follows.

6.1.1 Step 1: Be Credible

Think of LinkedIn as your very own personal website. The first step, then, is to ensure that you are credible when and if a prospect were to visit your profile. That is, you are who you say you are and appear to be someone who can help them. You should have an up-to-date profile that includes the following:

- A nice background (i.e., company colors or branding)
- A professional headshot (i.e., how you would appear if a prospect were to meet you)
- A relevant yet provocative headline
- Up-to-date working experience
- Relevant content

Note: You must post and/or share relevant content to keep your profile active. Remember that a prospect is likely to visit your profile, so there should be something there to view that reassures them you are who you say you are. Having an active presence does not have to be overly labor-intensive or complicated. You can share posts from your company, your existing customers or clients, and any other relevant information. For my B2B LinkedIn Prospect Posting Resource, visit www.unstoppablesalesprospecting.com.

6.1.2 Step 2: Earn Attention

You'll want to visit their profile to get your prospect's attention. The goal isn't to stalk them but rather to visit once. In doing so, you'll assess if they are active on LinkedIn (do they like, comment on, or create their posts? Do they have a profile picture? Is their work experience up to date?, etc.). If they are not, consider using a different form of communication.

More importantly, if your profile isn't hidden from public view, your prospect will see that you visited their profile. This is a good thing, as it brings awareness to who you are, and the chances are they will, in turn, visit your profile to "check you out." If what they find is relevant (i.e., see Step 1), then they will deem you credible.

6.1.3 Step 3: Engage

Once you have visited their profile, wait 24–48 hours, and send a cold connection request (i.e., without a personalized message). Yes, this goes against much of what you've likely heard about LinkedIn but hear me out. My studies have found almost no difference in whether your connection request will be accepted, whether you send a personalized message, and if your profile is up to date, following the steps outlined above. So why waste time attempting to come up with the perfect message? For those who don't accept your connection request within 30 days, withdraw it, and you can resend one (there is a waiting period of three weeks as of this writing). For these, I suggest you retry using a personalized and relevant message.

6.1.4 Step 4: Add Value

Your goal in connecting on any platform is to add value by providing your prospects with resources, support, ideas, samples, assessments, and market insights, all to support them in their research. Your primary goal in providing value is to become a trusted advisor to your prospect, someone they deem an expert in the area you specialize in, and therefore, critical to helping your prospect make an informed decision. Your tertiary goal is to promote your product or service by providing such resources.

In other words, you want to become someone your prospect deems they need to follow, connect with, and speak to if they're going to make an informed decision about purchasing your products or services. On LinkedIn, for example, you might share articles, assessments, invites to groups, invitations to special events, etc., all designed to assist your prospect in making an informed buying decision that includes you as part of the equation.

6.1.5 Step 5: Suggest a Discussion

Once you've connected on LinkedIn, are seen as credible, and have provided value to your prospect, your goal should be to suggest a brief discussion. Many sales professionals I've encountered are too direct on LinkedIn. They send a message and immediately suggest a meeting as soon as they connect. Think of this as dating; you must form trust before you ask to go out, and the same applies here. Remember, your prospects are being pitched daily on LinkedIn, so you need to set yourself apart from your competition and all the LinkedIn trolls out there. The discussion stage is typically best completed *after* three weeks (or more) of engagement on LinkedIn. Here is an example of a timeline to follow to reach the point of suggesting a discussion.

> **Week 1:** Send cold connection request; connection accepted; reply to the connection (i.e., "Great to connect Greg.")
>
> **Week 2:** Share value (i.e., a relevant article). Keep language informal: "Hi Sara, I thought you might appreciate this article on X."
>
> **Week 3:** Share more value (i.e., send an assessment) to be useful. "Sara, this assessment is something our clients have used to ensure they aren't overpaying for their commercial insurance. Wanted to share it in hopes you find it useful.")
>
> **Week 4:** Suggest Discussion. "Hi Sara, I'm not sure if you had a chance to look at the assessment I sent along. However, I'm happy to connect for a few minutes to share how our best clients have used it to reduce their commercial insurance costs."

You would continue sharing value and suggesting a conversation, alternating between the two until you receive a response. A good rule of thumb is to send a message every other week initially, or better yet, you can apply the accelerated touchpoint approach discussed earlier in this book.

6.2 LINKEDIN MESSAGING: THE NEW INBOX

In my LinkedIn prospecting strategy above, you'll notice that I do not suggest you "like" or "comment" on your prospect's posts. You can do this if you'd like, but as mentioned earlier, I find this a black hole that can absorb more of your precious time than it's worth. Also, our goal is prospecting, which is active outreach and pursuit rather than passive liking or commenting.

If you incorporate something else to warm up prospects, that's fine, but in my experience, this approach is more assertive and effective. LinkedIn has become the replacement inbox for many prospects whose real email inboxes are overflowing and who have spam filters slowly filtering out their cold emails. For those prospects who use LinkedIn, it offers a direct line of communication uninfluenced by outside forces such as IT or company policy. Is every one of your prospects on LinkedIn? No. Is everyone going to engage on LinkedIn? Also, no. But you can be sure that those who connect have a strong opportunity to engage in a discussion.

For this reason, there is a golden rule you should go by when using LinkedIn. If someone engages on the platform with you in a discussion, do not, I repeat, do not move off the platform until they suggest so or you deem it necessary. For example, if someone connects, don't email them; expect them to respond. Or if someone sends you a message, don't expect them to pick up the phone. Part of your ability to influence a prospect is to communicate with them on the channel they prefer to communicate with you on. Suppose a prospect engages with you on a channel. In that case, they are telling you that is where they are most comfortable communicating, so stay with that channel until they suggest you move (i.e., "send me an email") or you need to move (i.e., "Can I send you an invitation via email?").

6.3 AUTOMATION AS A TOOL, NOT A CRUTCH

You'll notice that nowhere in this chapter have I mentioned using automation. Plenty of software platforms can assist you with LinkedIn outreach, sending automated messages and responses on your behalf. There are a few reasons I recommend shying away from this. First, LinkedIn, like many social platforms such as Facebook, Instagram, etc., can often identify the use of automation software; to be blunt, they don't like it. I've met sales professionals who lost access to their profiles because of being identified as using automation software. If you decide to automate anywhere, do so at your own risk and recognize you might lose access to the platform. Secondly, I'm not against automation, but you need to develop an effective system or method before you introduce automation. Don't assume what a software company provides will be adequate for you and your needs.

It's old-school thinking, but I've found that sales professionals have become eager to introduce automation (believing it will work for them). Then, they let automation do the initial outreach and messaging, only to lose track of emerging conversations. When you put your "system" before "technology," you get clear on what works, and in turn, this informs your pursuit of any software to support your efforts.

Lastly, prospecting requires a level of creativity on your end. It requires you to assess what's working, what's not, and what to do about it. When you turn over the "thinking" aspect to software, you lose the discipline and focus to think for yourself. Your goal should always be to find software that can help you determine what already works but do it more effectively or efficiently.

Where technology becomes advantageous when using LinkedIn is through its native platform, Sales Navigator.[24] We will cover some basic features of Sales Navigator here. However, I'd strongly suggest you check it out for yourself to determine if it will benefit you. Remember what we said earlier: LinkedIn has over 800 million active users as of this writing, so any tool they provide is most often your best means of accessing prospects and other functionality. Additionally, when you use LinkedIn's platform, you avoid any risks of LinkedIn shutting you down. Lastly, LinkedIn Sales Navigator does have an additional cost of about $100/month for access to the features we'll discuss, so be aware that there is a cost to using this platform.

Find Prospects: One of the benefits I appreciate about the Sales Navigator platform is the ability to search, filter, and sort contacts. You can define the exact stats for the prospects you seek (i.e., industry, sector, region, business size, title) and then build groups of contacts.

Make Contact: The platform allows you to send InMail's (a form of direct message sent directly to your prospect's LinkedIn account) to prospects, and there are options to use dynamic data to identify optimum timing for your messages. As of this writing, new AI features are also being added to further assist in finding leads and automating messaging.

Conversation Preparation: Sales Navigator lets you capture and summarize key information about prospects using AI, helping you understand prospective accounts and quickly prepare for meetings and discussions. There is also software that provides buyer intent signals, allowing you to know when the right time is to reach out or follow up with prospects.

These are just an overview of the benefits of Sales Navigator and by no means are meant to suggest that using the platform will lead to prospecting success. As mentioned earlier, you need to create a prospecting system first, and then identify what technology will help you improve the efficiency and effectiveness of that system. But if you are using or plan to use LinkedIn as part of your research and/or outreach methods, then Sales Navigator might be a tool in your toolbox.

Now that we've covered three foundational channels for prospecting, let's dive into some more advanced techniques that you can use to help you improve your prospecting results and accelerate your success.

UNSTOPPABLE SALES PROSPECTING SYSTEM ACTION STEP

What improvements should you make to your LinkedIn profile? How can you become more active to demonstrate your credibility? How will you incorporate LinkedIn messaging as part of your outreach strategy?

Part Three

Prospecting Strategies to Differentiate from Your Competition

In the previous chapters, we've discussed some basic prospecting methods foundational in B2B sales. Now, it's time to dive deeper or peel back the onion, as the saying goes, to uncover additional, more complex strategies to support building up your Unstoppable Sales^{SM} Prospecting System.

Top sales performers always seek ways to expand their reach and bring new prospects into their pipeline. For you to do the same, think about prospecting as an ecosystem consisting of a series of rings with contact points along each ring. Diagram 7.1 demonstrates the prospecting ecosystem.

For example, the outer ring, which is farthest from your prospect, will include communication methods that are differentiated from your competition and require little effort on the part of your prospect. As you get closer to the prospect, communication channels become more intimate and less differentiated.

DOI: 10.4324/9781003604457-9

Prospecting Ecosystem

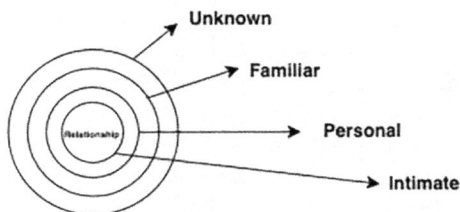

DIAGRAM 7.1
Prospecting Ecosystem.

Through the prospecting strategies we'll discuss in this chapter, you'll begin forming these outer rings, slowly working toward the inner part of the circle. As you do, you'll increase the awareness of your ideal prospects about who you are and how you can help, and in turn, you'll continuously expand your prospect pipeline. Most importantly, the strategies discussed in this section will further differentiate you from your competition, helping you stand out from others in your segment.

7

If All Else Fails – Use Direct Mail

When you read this title, you'll likely want to skip this chapter, dismissing direct mail as something only marketing can or should do. Please discard this assumption for three reasons.

1. Your goal in prospecting is to stand out and differentiate yourself from your competition. It's unlikely they are sending direct mail.
2. Events such as technology, the pandemic, and unpredictable postal disruptions continue to diminish the amount of physical mail people receive. As a result, direct mail is a channel you can use to gain direct access to your prospects.
3. When did you last receive physical mail and didn't open it? Direct mail, when done correctly, unlike most email, gets opened and read.

If you have a marketing team, you can partner with them on this. However, you won't need them to execute what we will discuss in this chapter. Moreover, your goal is to make direct mail very informal and personalized, so investing in some big outreach campaigns is not what I suggest. Instead, direct mail for our purposes will include things like special reports, cards, letters, and brochures with personalized notes. Remember, before you engage a prospect, you need to earn their attention, and sending physical mail can be a great strategy.

DOI: 10.4324/9781003604457-10

7.1 DIRECT MAIL: YOUR KEY TO DIFFERENTIATION

To begin with, let's consider some statistics that pertain to direct mail and its impact:

- A survey by Statista found that 65% of Gen Y and 57% of Gen Z respondents were excited to receive a piece of direct mail.[25]
- According to the Print & Mail Communications Association, direct mail has an open rate of 42.2%.[25]
- HBR has reported that 49% of businesses see an increase in sales and inquiries when they send an email along with a catalog.[25]

I've selected these studies because they highlight some important observations about using direct mail. Direct mail significantly impacts all generations; the open rates are substantially higher than other forms of media, such as email, and when coupled with different communication methods, it can enhance the overall interest and inquiries from prospective clients or customers.

Most importantly, consider that your competitors are unlikely to use direct mail, or if they do, they turn the function over to marketing to run. As someone who picked up this book seeking new and more effective ways to connect with prospects, you can likely see the opportunity this creates.

Your goal is to consider the kinds of direct mail you might use as part of your outreach to prospects and at what point using direct mail makes sense. Let's begin with some examples of direct mail you might consider, as follows:

- A letter to a prospect
- Brochures or other marketing materials (with a personalized note)
- Postcards
- A relevant study or statistics as it pertains to your product, service, or company
- A pertinent article from an online or offline source (with a personalized note)
- Holiday, birthday, or greeting cards
- A survey
- A product sample, photo, or special component
- Video players or USB sticks with a video on them

The options are endless; however, the key is personalizing each item to the prospect and their unique situation. For example, I don't suggest you send a marketing brochure or article without including a handwritten personalized note that accompanies it. If your handwriting is poor, you can create customized messages and sign them with your name. Websites like Canva.com can be great for this.

With so many options for using direct mail, the next step is to determine when and how best to introduce direct mail as part of your prospecting process. The good news is that in my experience, there is no wrong way to incorporate direct mail; in other words, I haven't met a sales or business development professional using direct mail who has had a problem because of sending it at the wrong time in their prospecting process.

Consider the following options to assess when and how to introduce direct mail in your prospecting process.

1. As an introductory letter to you and your company.
2. As a follow-up to your initial outreach (via another communication channel) attempt to engage the prospect.
3. To reinforce the benefits of your product or service (i.e., share customer or client testimonials).
4. To aid in the understanding of the unique features of your product or service (i.e., sending a sample or a unique feature of your product or service).
5. As a thank-you for the response to your email or connection (i.e., thank-you card).
6. Pre-meeting to minimize the chances of cancellation (i.e., reinforce the benefits of your product or service and what the prospect will gain through participation in the upcoming meeting).

To identify when and how to use direct mail in your prospecting process, consider the following questions:

1. Where might a direct mail piece help to accelerate your impact on a prospect?
2. How can you use direct mail to differentiate yourself from the competition?
3. What can you send to reinforce the benefits and value you and your products or services can provide?

4. How easily can you access and/or create the direct mail piece (i.e., you'll want to make this a standard piece customized for each prospect)?

With these questions answered, let's discuss strategies to ensure direct mail gets into your prospect's hands rather than being stopped at the front desk or mailroom!

7.2 USING DIRECT MAIL TO GET PAST A GATEKEEPER

The benefits of using direct mail as part of your prospecting process are numerous; however, for our purposes, let's recap three of the most important.

1. Direct mail can set you apart from your closest competitor (who isn't using direct mail) and help you differentiate yourself (which, if you haven't figured it out by now, is a key to earning your prospect's attention).
2. Direct mail offers direct communication to your prospect and won't get stuck in a spam filter or cyberspace.
3. Direct mail can get you past gatekeepers, who may otherwise screen your emails, phone calls, and visits to prospects.

Getting past the gatekeeper doesn't automatically happen if you use direct mail. There are some steps to take to ensure this happens. However, when taken, your chances of your mail being opened and read by your prospect increase exponentially. Also, it's important to mention that you must be creative to ensure a gatekeeper doesn't discard your direct mail.

First, let's clarify who some of the common gatekeepers may be that you'll encounter; they include:

- Administrative Assistants
- Executive Assistants
- Office Managers
- Receptionists
- Decision-Influencers (those who influence the decision-maker)

The role of these gatekeepers is simple: to filter out those who intend to waste your prospect's time. Unfortunately for us in sales, gatekeepers often assume that salespeople fall into the "time wasters" category, so they will discard our mail if they sense we are in sales or trying to sell something.

Additionally, gatekeepers are often concerned about filtering personal mail for decision-makers. Have you ever opened a piece of mail and realized it was for someone else? You immediately put the mail back into the envelope and rushed it to the person it was intended for. This is what happens when gatekeepers sense a piece of mail is of a personal nature for a decision-maker.

There are three options when it comes to dealing with a gatekeeper who is likely to screen your direct mail:

> **Option 1:** Address the mail to the gatekeeper, requesting it be forwarded to the decision-maker on your behalf.
> **Option 2:** Address the mail to the decision-maker and take steps to ensure the gatekeeper passes it along.
> **Option 3:** Address the mail to the gatekeeper and decision-maker in parallel.

Which option you choose will depend on how closely the gatekeeper works with the decision-maker, their relationship, what level of responsibility the gatekeeper is assigned in filtering out mail for the decision-maker, and how seriously they take their job.

If you are unsure, call the decision-maker's office, intending to speak with the gatekeeper, advising you have a package to send to the decision-maker, and asking how to deliver it best. They will likely ask which company you are with and your name, which you should openly share. If they ask what the package is, say it's some information for the decision-maker. The response you get from the gatekeeper will tell you just how serious they are about their job and give you hints as to which option you should pursue.

With this in mind, let's identify the common steps you should take to ensure your mail passes the gatekeeper.

7.3 STEPS TO ENSURE YOUR DIRECT MAIL GETS PAST A GATEKEEPER

1. Address your direct mail to the decision-maker – using their full name (Ms. Susan Smith).

2. Use an oversized envelope with stamps (don't use a postal machine, if possible, as it can appear less personalized).
3. Include your return address without your company name.
4. Consider sending the direct mail via a courier (i.e., FedEx will often be forwarded to a decision-maker without ever being opened).
5. Use a professional tone rather than being overly promotional. If the gatekeeper does open your mail, there's a better chance they will forward it.

If you choose, you can add a sticker to the envelope that says, "Private and Confidential." If you hesitate to do this, consider that this is true (your goal is for the decision-maker to read the piece), and there is a chance that this will deter any gatekeeper from reading your mail.

With these tips in mind, let's identify the best ways to integrate direct mail into your prospect outreach.

7.4 INTEGRATING DIRECT MAIL INTO YOUR PROSPECT OUTREACH

I'm hopeful you will see that direct mail is a direct channel through which you can reach your ideal prospects. It's also a path less traveled by most of your competition, offering you a captive audience and a means of differentiating yourself and your offer.

As mentioned, if you want to work with your marketing team to develop various assets (that your prospects would find valuable) to share, suit yourself; however, it's unnecessary. You can easily do this and get better results because it will have a greater impact when coming from you. For example, a handwritten note direct from you will have a greater influence on your prospect's desire to connect with you than some promotional material that marketing has put together. No slight against marketing intended, just an observation after years of helping sales teams develop prospecting systems. Personalization trumps aesthetics every time (read that statement twice!).

Here are the steps you should take to introduce and integrate direct mail into your prospecting system.

7.5 SHAWN'S DIRECT MAIL PROSPECTING SYSTEM

1 **Identify what you will send as a direct mail piece:** Depending on the outcome of your answer to number one above, you can assess what you will send with the most significant impact. Some examples to get you started may include an introductory letter, a customer testimonial, a brochure with a handwritten note attached, an assessment, an invitation to an exclusive event, etc. The options are endless, so don't get caught up in finding the perfect resource to send; instead, test sending something to five prospects and then determine its impact. Remember, your goal here is to earn some awareness, so if you get a response, your direct mail was successful.

2 **Identify when you will send a direct mail piece to your prospects:** Is it the first piece of information you want to send to introduce yourself, or something you will send later in your outreach once more traditional methods (i.e., email and telephone) have failed to produce a response? I have a colleague who sent a personalized letter and a seedling to every prospect, suggesting how he could help them grow their business. Alternatively, several clients who send handwritten notes after initial outreach via email and phone have failed. Test out direct mail at different stages of your prospecting process to determine what has the most significant impact.

3 **Determine how you will follow up:** Once you've sent a direct mail piece, you'll want to follow up to ensure it arrived and assess its impact. My suggestion is to make a phone call approximately three business days after you expect the direct mail, ask the prospect if they received the information you sent. You can take this one step further and mention in your piece a date/time you will call them to ensure its arrival – which can prepare the prospect for your call. What's important here isn't so much that you confirm arrival, but instead, you have a reason to contact your prospect again, without it being the same old message (i.e., do you have some time to speak with me, to meet).

4 **Determine how you will send the direct mail:** As mentioned previously, you'll want to take steps to ensure your direct mail gets past the gatekeeper, so it's essential to determine how you will send the mail piece. Some companies specialize in sending direct mail (search "direct mail providers" in Google to find one nearest to you, or nearest to

your prospects if it makes more sense), or you can keep it simple and purchase some 4″ × 5″ cards and envelopes and mail them yourself. However, I suggest sending via courier or expected mail (I refer to this as the gold standard). When you take this step, there is a greater chance your mail will make it directly to the decision-maker. You can even purchase some stickers online that say things like "confidential information" or "urgent" that you can add. Fair warning, though: your goal is to make this appear as a professional piece, not a piece of spam mail that the gatekeeper (or decision-maker) throws out, so be careful if you start adding stickers or anything that makes the mail appear as junk.

5 **Determine your budget:** Depending on how many prospects you are attempting to reach, what you intend to mail, and how you plan to send the mail, the cost may be a consideration. If you are sending these at scale and have decided to use a company to handle the design, print, and distribution, get an estimate of the price before you launch them in direct mail. You'll need to have the budget available to do so. Personalized and straightforward often impact more than professional pieces you may have designed and sent. One of the most significant impacts of direct mail I've encountered is when sales professionals send a 4″ × 5″ card with a handwritten note. You can scale direct mail; however, you can also keep it simple and highly cost-effective. It all depends on how far you want to go with it as part of your prospecting strategy.

Now that we've uncovered how to use direct mail to reach your decision-makers strategically, let's discuss something that's becoming a more common prospecting strategy but is also being abused. Jump over to Chapter 8, and I'll see you there!

UNSTOPPABLE SALES PROSPECTING SYSTEM ACTION STEP

How can you integrate direct mail into your prospecting to differentiate yourself? What value can you share via direct mail? How will you ensure what you send is personalized and makes it to the decision-maker?

8

Strategies for Using Text Messages in Prospecting

There are varying opinions on whether text messaging, otherwise known as short message service (SMS), is an appropriate channel for reaching out to cold prospects.

Depending on the country in which your prospect resides, sometimes regulations govern when and how you can reach out to a prospect who doesn't know you are using channels such as text message, email, and telephone. Where such regulations exist, they often have to do with the consent of the receiver of your messages, specifically when consent is necessary, how to attain it, and what represents consent. These regulations most commonly require explicit consent from the receiver and a clear and simple method to opt out of your communications. These can vary by country, so research and know the regulations before you start any cold outreach.

Before we dive into methods of using text messaging as part of your prospecting, let me share a few things about how to best incorporate this as part of your Unstoppable Sales^SM Prospecting System. First, I'm not a fan of reaching out to prospects cold using text messages, so for this reason, it's not a primary outreach method you'll hear me discuss. I'm confident some of you reading this have successfully sent cold text messages, and that's great – but it's not what I recommend considering the varying other options at your disposal. I recommend that you use text messaging to follow up with a prospect once you have made initial contact and spoken. My perspective may change on this in the future, considering shifts in prospects' demographics (i.e., younger prospects are much more comfortable with cold text messages); however, as of this writing, it's not something I recommend.

Also, let's clarify how text messaging was intended to be used. SMS stands for short message service, with a heavy emphasis on "short." If you send a text message that is more than two sentences in length, you shouldn't be using text messaging. Like other communication platforms we have discussed and will be discussing, the goal of using a text message to earn your prospect's attention. You achieve this by sending short, personalized messages or videos. If you tend to send lengthy messages via text message, email, or LinkedIn, then challenge yourself, using the scripts and examples we're discussing in this book, to develop shorter, punchier, and more appealing messages.

Lastly, like other forms of prospect communication, your text message is intended to get a response. Due to the brief nature of text messaging, you must ensure the message you send is a question or ends with one. For example, you might send a text message to confirm a meeting with a prospect they've already accepted that says, "Krista, confirming you are still good to connect at 10 am this morning?" or a text message to ensure an emailed document was received: "Morning Brian, did you receive the survey results I sent by email?" Notice these suggest you have already connected with the prospect.

Now that you understand how text messaging will complement your prospecting process, let's explore some specific strategies you can implement immediately.

8.1 WHO IS THIS? DO I KNOW YOU?

For this book, we'll discuss SMS and WhatsApp simultaneously as our primary "texting" tools. SMS text messaging (using a smartphone) became popular in the early 2000s, with WhatsApp being launched shortly thereafter, in 2009. Today, both platforms offer users similar features (Interesting Fact: WhatsApp was intended to track users' work statuses and notify their contacts when they were available). Based on my experience, one distinction to note is that WhatsApp is the preferred means of communication in some parts of the world, whereas SMS texting is more preferred in others. For example, in my work with sales teams in Mexico, the United Kingdom, Chile, and South Africa, WhatsApp is the preferred means of communication compared to SMS messaging. Alternatively, in North America, SMS texting is preferred over WhatsApp. If you are unsure which method your prospects choose, ask them during initial conversations. Note that you can replicate the strategies we'll discuss in this book on both platforms.

An important point to mention is that most users use SMS or WhatsApp for more personal relationships and for what they deem to be essential communications. If you open your phone right now, you likely have a long list of contacts with whom you have a personalized relationship or cherish a direct connection. For example, on my phone, I have a long list of friends and family members in my SMS and WhatsApp, as well as some long-term clients.

What you won't find in most people's SMS or WhatsApp is a list of strangers or people they don't know. When one such message arrives, both applications make it easy to swipe, delete, or delete and block, ensuring the number doesn't land in your message box again. In other words, blocking or "unsubscribing" from someone's communication whom you don't recognize is even easier on these platforms than in email and most social media platforms. I recommend avoiding these until you have connected with the prospect. We certainly don't want you blocked before you get started!

Still not convinced text messaging is best saved for after you've had a meaningful interaction with a prospect? If you are a professional salesperson (which I presume you are if you reading this book), then selling is based on building trust with a prospect. The attention you seek from your prospect is something that you want to earn. There is a distinct difference between achieving your prospect's attention and getting their attention. Getting attention is something that advertisers attempt to do through repeated and sometimes shocking or humorous ads.

For example, ads designed to stop viewers from drinking and driving sometimes show disturbing images of vehicle accidents; Burger King ran an ad that showed a moldy Whopper hamburger, demonstrating that their burgers were free of preservatives, etc. Shock advertising can effectively get attention from existing (well-known) brands. However, you are reaching out to someone who doesn't know you, possibly doesn't know your company, and with whom you intend to build a long-term, trusted relationship. Shock or an unexpected (and unwelcomed) surprise will not help you achieve your objectives.

Throughout this book, I discuss the importance of being provocative and differentiating yourself from the competition. You will do so through your language and the value and information you share. Sending an SMS message doesn't support differentiation in a good way, and it's possible that many of your prospects may see you as an unwelcomed intrusion if they don't yet know you, which can be very difficult to bounce back from.

If you have used text messaging or WhatsApp as part of your sales prospecting, it's likely that at some point you've received a response to your message that said, "Who is this? Do I know you?" This is not the best starting point for a trusted relationship with a prospect. Consider text messaging as a secondary communication channel rather than a primary channel.

With this in mind, let's consider incorporating SMS and/or WhatsApp into your Unstoppable Sales^{SM} Prospecting System.

8.2 TEXTING AS A PROSPECTING TOOL

Due to the more personalized nature of text messaging, in my experience working with sales teams globally, there is a better chance of a response once you and the prospect have had an initial interaction or conversation. You've spoken on the phone, had a virtual meeting, or met in person. The lengthier that interaction (i.e., a one-hour meeting vs. a five-minute introduction at an event), the better your chances of getting a response.

To clarify, having a conversation does not mean they replied to your initial outreach email; rather, you've had an interaction that allowed you to ask some questions, learn more about them, and understand their goals or objectives as they relate to your product or service. Diagram 8.1 demonstrates when this occurs in the sales conversation.

Prospecting Ecosystem Progression

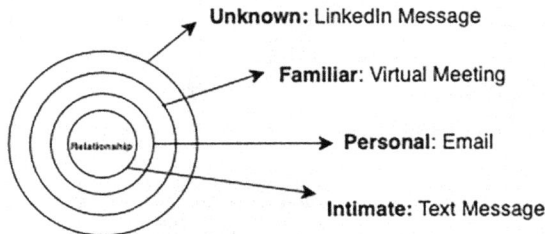

DIAGRAM 8.1
Prospecting Ecosystem Progression.

There are a few instances when using SMS or WhatsApp as a primary method to reach out to a prospect makes sense, as follows:

1. **It's Your Prospect's Preference**: If a prospect sends you a text message, that's a sign that it's the communication channel they prefer. In this instance, apply the logic outlined in point number 3.
2. **Other Communication Channels Haven't Yielded a Response**: If you are attempting to re-engage a prospect (i.e., you've met or had a conversation; however, the prospect has now dropped off and is unavailable), then you might consider sending an SMS or WhatsApp as an attempt to re-engage them. As discussed earlier in this chapter, just be aware of any regulations governing cold outreach in the prospective country.
3. **As part of a Marketing Outreach Campaign**: In some situations, it may make sense to send a text message as part of a cold outreach campaign. These are campaigns put together by marketing and a means of reaching out based on a specific event or circumstance. For example, you could send a cold text (SMS) message to prospective customers who attended an event you participated in or send a text message to a list of prospects with whom you haven't spoken but who opted in to receive such communications. Participating in these marketing campaigns may make sense depending on what you sell and with whom you deal. However, if your name is used as the message's sender, it may create some unwanted awareness of who you are and what you sell. If you have a marketing department or firm that wants to use these types of campaigns, think twice before letting your name be the sender, as it's something you'll carry with you that could cause you some problems later.

With these in mind, let's turn our attention to the best ways to structure your text messages to prospects with whom you've already connected.

8.3 STRUCTURING A PROSPECT TEXT MESSAGE

I have a distant relative who is what I refer to as a single-word texter. Each text or SMS message he sends consists of one or two words. If you have notifications on or these messages pop onto your screen, it isn't enjoyable and not how your prospects want to be perceived. Alternatively, you likely know someone who sends lengthy, long-winded, multi-sentence SMS or WhatsApp messages, which is equally annoying.

To avoid annoying your prospect, let's examine the best structure and language to use in your SMS or WhatsApp messages for the most significant impact.

There are several rules for effective text messaging that you will already have picked up from this chapter, namely, to keep your SMS or WhatsApp messages brief and include a question to entice a response (often referred to as a "call to action"). Here is a more robust list of guidelines for structuring an effective SMS or WhatsApp message.

Guidelines for Structuring an Effective SMS or WhatsApp Message:

1 Begin with a Personalized Introduction (i.e., "Hi John" or "John").
2 Confirm Your Name as the Sender (i.e., the prospect may not have your name on their phone).
3 Keep the Message Brief (i.e., a maximum of 160 characters in preview mode).
4 Ask a Relevant (and Essential) Question: "Are you still good to meet on Friday at 10 am?"
5 Provide Value and Reasoning: "I have a new product sample I'd be excited to show you."

Here are some examples of what a message might look like using the guidelines above:

Example 1:

"Hi Sara, it's Shawn. Are you planning to be in the office Friday? I have a sample of our widget to drop off."

Example 2:

"Hi Ryan, it's Shawn Casemore. Did you receive the package I sent? It contained some further information about our product."

Example 3:

"John, it's Shawn Casemore. Are we still good to meet tomorrow? I have some new ideas from my operations team to share."

To this point, we've discussed using text in our messages; however, before ending this chapter, let's discuss frequently asked questions about the use and application of SMS or WhatsApp.

Frequently Asked Questions about SMS and WhatsApp for B2B Sales Prospecting:

1. When should I use video or audio messages over text messages?: To begin with, although video and audio are often proven to convert (i.e., get a response) better than text, using SMS or WhatsApp is an exception. Your goal should always be to select the mode that makes the most sense for the message. In other words, sending a text or audio message would make sense if you already have a strong relationship with a prospect. Alternatively, if your relationship is still in its infancy, a video message might make more sense to reacquaint or familiarize your prospect with who you are. Numerous studies support video conversation better than text.[26]

2. Should I include images with my SMS or WhatsApp Message?: There's an old saying: a picture is worth a thousand words. Include one if the message you send is more powerful using an image. If you follow my guidelines to this point and are using SMS or WhatsApp as part of Phase 2 of your prospecting communication, then an image can increase both the relevance to the reader and the chances of a quick response. Revisiting my sample messages above, let's look at how you might include an image to improve your chances of a response:

Example 1:

"Hi Sara, it's Shawn. Are you planning to be in the office Friday? I have a sample of our widget to drop off." Action Step: Include a picture of the widget.

Example 2:

"Hi Ryan, it's Shawn Casemore. Did you receive the package I sent? It contained some further information about our product." Action Step: Include a photo of the original package sent.

Example 3:

"John, it's Shawn Casemore. Are we still good to meet tomorrow? I have some new ideas from my operations team to share." Action Step: Include a photo of an email from Operations.

You can see how an image can almost always improve the relevance and value of the information sent. Referring to my earlier point about multiple messages, avoid the urge to send multiple images – rather, just send one.

3. Should I Use WhatsApp Instead of SMS Text Messages?: In my experience, preferences for WhatsApp over Text Messaging are first dependent on where you are located (i.e., in Mexico, the use of WhatsApp is more commonplace than in Canada as of this writing) and second, depending on the receiver's preferences. For this reason, when you connect with a prospect (i.e., face-to-face meeting, virtual meeting), ask their preference. For example: "Susan, if it's easier to share that information via message, would you prefer text or WhatsApp?"

Now that we've covered the best applications and uses of SMS and WhatsApp as part of your prospecting system, let's dive into your prospect meetings – specifically, how to ensure they are effective and maintain momentum in your prospecting process.

UNSTOPPABLE SALES PROSPECTING SYSTEM ACTION STEP

How are you using SMS text messaging or WhatsApp in your prospect communications? What changes or improvements should you make to ensure their use is more effective? What stage might you use text messaging consistently to accelerate your prospect conversations?

9

In-Person Meetings Are Different

Depending on what you sell, in-person meetings may or may not make sense. The general rule I like to apply is that the higher the value of the product or service you sell, the more likely you are to use in-person meetings to build a trusted relationship and improve your chances of converting the sale.

Suppose in-person meetings are part of your prospecting process today, or you are considering having more. In that case, this chapter will help you improve the efficiency and effectiveness of those meetings as part of your overall prospecting process. For example, for those of you using in-person meetings already, we'll discuss some strategies to make your meetings more effective; for those who aren't using in-person meetings, we'll uncover the best ways to incorporate them into your prospecting to improve your chances of winning the sale.

Let's begin by discussing in-person meeting goals as part of your prospecting process.

9.1 MYTHS ABOUT COLD DROP-INS

Myth #1: Increased Company Security Makes Drop-in Meetings Impossible: There is some truth to the fact that some companies have put greater protocols into place for security, heavily influenced during the pandemic to control visitors; however, in my experience and that of many of those I train, most of these protocols are no longer followed. For example, there may be a restriction on visitors who don't have appointments. However, this doesn't stop you from connecting with your prospect – more on how to make such an attempt and some options for language in just a moment.

DOI: 10.4324/9781003604457-12

Myth #2: Prospects Work from Home, so Drop-in Meetings Don't Work: There have indeed been an increased number of people who work from home since 2020. However, since this time, most companies have requested, or even demanded, that employees return to the office at least part-time. Numerous studies have shown that there is a growing expectation of CEOs that their employees return to work, and additional studies have shown even younger generations are seeking employment where in-office experiences exist.[27] Additionally, if you are selling to a position that is at the executive level, they almost always spend at least some days each week in their office.

Myth #3: Stopping by Unannounced Upsets Most Prospects: This reason is often not based on fact but opinion. Possibly you've had the experience of stopping by to visit a prospect unannounced, and either they don't come to see you in person (i.e., "Sorry, John's in a meeting right now and can't meet with you."), or you've had the experience of a prospect telling you they don't appreciate or accept "drop-ins." The latter is rare but can happen (ask me how I know). The reality is that there are far fewer instances where a prospect may not appreciate your drop-in or agree to meet with you despite being available than you might think. Most prospects will give you time if you stop by to see them, recognizing that you invested time and effort (and possibly traveled a distance).

There are some criteria to consider when confirming if including cold drop-ins in your prospecting process will be a good strategy for you, as follows:

1. Your product or service is a high-dollar value item.
2. Your prospects are in a focused geographic area that you can reach with relative ease.
3. Your best prospect conversions happen because of in-person discussions.
4. Competitors use mainly virtual methods (i.e., email and video) to connect with prospects.
5. You sell a highly complex or technical product or service.
6. Drop-ins are convenient for you, given your proximity to your prospects.

If some of these criteria align with your circumstances, then using cold drop-ins as part of your initial prospect outreach is something you should be practicing. The next logical question is how to position the drop-in for the most significant impact. Fortunately, you can include several different yet highly effective drop-in strategies in your prospecting process. Below, I'll describe each, when to use them, and how to ensure each is effective.

9.2 YOUR GOAL WHEN MEETING IN-PERSON

When it comes to building your unstoppable sales prospecting system, I suggest using a hybrid approach to your meetings where possible, that is to start with either a virtual meeting or phone call to qualify both the interest of your prospect and their ability to buy. This ensures that moving to an in-person meeting only happens once you've confirmed the time and effort is warranted (i.e., you've qualified the buyer and their interest in your product or service). This isn't always possible, however, and when you are traveling to meet with prospects, it can be a good use of your time to stop in to meet with and pre-qualify other potential prospects if they are along your route.

There are numerous ways in-person meetings can be used as part of the prospecting process, for example:

Pre-Relationship Meeting: Stopping by to meet a prospect face-to-face with whom you've had no interaction or previous relationship with the goal of introducing yourself, your product, or your service.

Introductory Meeting: An in-person meeting held after an introduction to a prospect (i.e., you met at an event or were introduced virtually) to introduce yourself and your product or service and to learn more about the prospects company, needs, interests, etc.

Presentation Meeting: An in-person meeting in which you make a presentation to your prospect and others they deem important to attend the meeting to introduce your company, product, or service. *Note: A presentation meeting can also be an introductory meeting, with the difference being the salesperson is asked or requested to make a formal presentation.*

Discovery Meeting: This meeting most often occurs after an Introduction or Presentation meeting with the purpose of learning more about the prospect's specific needs, expectations, and objectives as they relate to your product or service.

Proposal Submission Meeting: This is a meeting, most often suggested by the salesperson, with the intention of reviewing a proposal or quotation before it is submitted. The objective is to ensure the proposal addresses everything learned about in the earlier discovery meeting and to share highlights and unique points that differentiate the proposal and offer from that of the competition.

Proposal Review Meeting: This is a meeting requested by the salesperson to review a proposal that's been submitted to ensure the prospect understands what's being proposed. These meetings are especially important when you are submitting a quote or proposal and competing against another company. The indirect goal of this meeting is to close the sale.

Attempt to Close Meeting: This meeting is often set when a quote or proposal has not yet closed, and attempts to do so virtually (i.e., via email, phone call) have been unsuccessful. The meeting is often described to the prospect as an "In the area" meeting, whereby the intent to close is not disclosed; rather, the meeting is out of convenience considering the salesperson is already near their office. Note: This is often not the case.

Post-Close Meeting: This is a meeting designed to quickly launch a new service or confirm details of the shipment of a product and follow a close. This meeting is particularly important if the purchase is complex or sensitive and allows the salesperson an opportunity to reconfirm important details and ensure the prospect is aware of what they have agreed to.

It's important to mention that any of these meetings can be converted to virtual, as was the case during the pandemic for many salespeople who were accustomed to in-person meetings. If you do so, however, be clear that virtual meetings simply don't have the same impact as in-person meetings. When you are in person with a prospect, there are fewer distractions for them to engage in, increasing their attention on you, and often resulting in a greater understanding of the information you share.

Not surprisingly, the goal of using any or all the in-person meetings listed above is to build trust and support prospect conversion. The challenging part, however, considering the different kinds of people you'll meet, and the logistics to coordinate in-person meetings, is how to build trust with each prospect.

In future chapters, we'll discuss how to increase the effectiveness of your virtual prospect meetings, but for now just know that in-person meetings can dramatically increase your conversion rates, particularly for complex, highly technical, and/or large investment products or services. For this reason, a goal of any in-person meeting is to take advantage of the improved communication opportunities using different forms of sharing information. In other words, don't just speak to, or ask questions of your prospect, take the opportunity to differentiate yourself by introducing various visual aids during your conversations. These can further increase trust and speed up the conversion process.

Examples of Aids to Improve In-Person Meeting Effectiveness

1. **Visual Aids**: Slides, brochures, line cards, drawings, graphs, charts, or other images.
2. **Kinesthetic Aids**: Product or Technical Demonstrations (i.e., video, physical, and online).
3. **Collaborative Aids**: Facility Tours, Assessments, 2 × 2 matrix.

Any or all these aids can be incorporated into in-person meetings to improve their effectiveness; however, the degree to which you use these will depend on what you sell. Additionally, the more you can engage prospects in using aids you can share, the greater the chances of building trust and accelerating prospect conversion. For example, I can show you an image, then engage you with a demonstration, or collaborate with you on completing an assessment. The more you can shift toward using collaborative aids with your prospect, where the prospect is using the aid rather than you, the better your chances of building and growing both trust and the relationship.

You'll also notice that not all the aids shared above can be used in a virtual meeting, which is another reason why in-person meetings can be more effective. They have a greater impact because of your ability to engage with and collaborate with your prospect. If you aren't using in-person meetings during your prospecting process, you sell a high-value and/or highly technical or complex product, and it's reasonable to consider traveling to and from a prospective customer within a day (i.e., a few hours of driving or a couple of hours on a plane), then I'd suggest you reconsider. It just might be the very thing that sets you apart from your competition.

9.3 THE DEATH OF 60-MINUTE MEETINGS

I can't put my finger on why; however, in my experience, many sales professionals continue to assume that 60-minute meetings are a goal when meeting with a prospect. They aren't. Time is your prospects most valuable resource, so we want to respect that time. More importantly, considering it's likely they want to give us very little of their precious time in the early stages of a relationship, by suggesting shorter meetings we achieve three things.

1. We make it easy for the prospect to say yes to a meeting with us.
2. We set ourselves apart from competitors who are always requesting longer meetings.
3. We force ourselves to focus on what's of greatest value to share with the prospect.

The golden rule I suggest you consider following when attempting to book meetings with your prospect is: Early meetings with a prospect should be 15–20 minutes in total and extend to 60 minutes only after the initial meetings to build trust are complete or at the direction of the prospect. Keeping in mind, of course, that if the prospect books an hour with you, suggests a longer meeting, or suggests extending the duration of a meeting, then you should take them up on the opportunity! However, when you are suggesting the time a meeting will take, shorter is better.

If you are traveling a significant distance to meet with a prospect, you might be thinking "but Shawn, this is a waste of time to meet in person if I only have 20 minutes!" The reality is, if the prospect knows the distance you are traveling, there is a good chance they will suggest a longer meeting (i.e., 60 minutes). Keep in mind though, it's not their problem you need to travel that far, so by initially suggesting a shorter meeting, even 30 minutes, your chances of their willingness to meet increase substantially.

Here is an example of the timing of your in-person prospect meetings:

1. Initial outreach to the prospect – request to speak with them for five (5) minutes.
2. After an initial conversation with a prospect – suggest a 20–30-minute follow-up meeting.
3. In the discovery and negotiation phase – book 30–45-minute meetings.
4. In the closing meeting – book 45–50-minute meetings.

Diagrams 9.1 and 9.2 demonstrates how these meetings roll out as part of your prospecting process.

Prospect Meeting Timeline

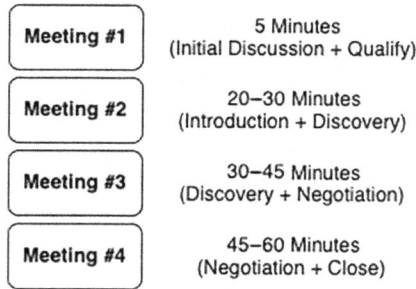

Meeting #1	5 Minutes (Initial Discussion + Qualify)
Meeting #2	20–30 Minutes (Introduction + Discovery)
Meeting #3	30–45 Minutes (Discovery + Negotiation)
Meeting #4	45–60 Minutes (Negotiation + Close)

DIAGRAM 9.1
Prospect Meeting Timeline.

Prospect Meeting Progression Timeline

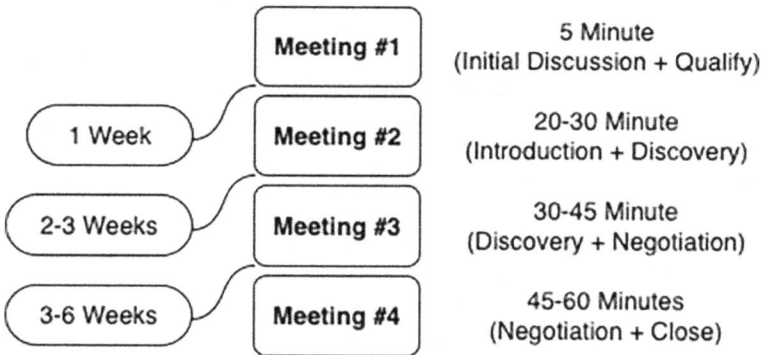

	Meeting #1	5 Minute (Initial Discussion + Qualify)
1 Week	Meeting #2	20-30 Minute (Introduction + Discovery)
2-3 Weeks	Meeting #3	30-45 Minute (Discovery + Negotiation)
3-6 Weeks	Meeting #4	45-60 Minutes (Negotiation + Close)

DIAGRAM 9.2
Prospect Meeting Progression with Timeline.

The reasons why you should use the timeline outlined above are as follows:

1. **Initial Meeting**: The goal is to convince the prospect to give you a few minutes of their time. Five minutes is something that virtually anyone can (and will) be willing to provide you. To ensure this time is effective, however, you'll need to have your initial messaging and questions tight. The goal of this meeting is to qualify the prospect.
2. **After Initial Meeting**: If the introductory meeting went well, your goal will be to get to know the prospect and their needs more. This is where a

lengthier meeting (20–30 minutes) comes into play. You'll start building a relationship in this meeting and share some basic (yet powerful) information with your prospect, while also asking some validating questions. The goal is to qualify the need (i.e., fit, timelines, decision-influencers).

3. **Discovery Meetings**: There is often more than one discovery meeting, and since these meetings are now with a qualified prospect who has a qualified need, the goal is to increase the length of the meeting to allow you sufficient time to ask questions, respond to questions, and ask follow-up questions. The length of 45 minutes allows your prospect the chance to wrap up with you and still have time to prepare for their next meeting. This is something you can mention if there is hesitation to hold the meeting due to time conflicts of your prospect. The goal of this meeting is to develop the framework for your quote or proposal.

4. **Proposal Review Meeting**: The goal of this meeting is to review unique attributes or areas of importance with your customer and attempt to close the opportunity. It's not uncommon to have a proposal review meeting as part of your sales process, as a means of addressing prospect questions, and ensuring clarity on what you propose or quote. Strategically, however, this meeting should be included to differentiate your offer from that of the competition and as a method of attempting to close the opportunity. Prior to issuing your quote or proposal, suggest to the prospect, "there are a few points in our quote that might cause some confusion, so let's book a few minutes to discuss next Tuesday." Getting this meeting booked on the calendar before you issue the quote can ensure you don't fall into the abyss and never hear back from the prospect.

5. **Closing Meeting**: This is often one or possibly two meetings, following your quote review meeting, and with the sole purpose of addressing any objections and closing the opportunity. Depending on the complexity of your offer, the number of meetings you need to hold post-proposal, and the number of objections you experience will differ; however, the objective of the meeting is still to close the opportunity.

If you are good at what you do, the reality is very few, if any, of these meetings require a full 60 minutes. Even in a scenario in which you are faced with numerous objections, questions, and clarifications, you are better to keep the meeting short (i.e., 45 minutes) and simply document the concerns, allowing you the chance to do some homework and respond accordingly.

If you wonder why I am so fixated on your keeping meeting times to less than 60 minutes let me remind you:

1. Your goal is to provide your prospect the ability to easily integrate your meetings into their day (lengthy meetings are harder to book for the day).
2. Leaving 10–15 minutes at the end of a meeting allows both yourself and the prospect to get prepared for their next meeting.
3. Meetings that drag on past 45 minutes tend to lose momentum and enthusiasm. You don't want a prospect to view you in this manner.

As with all meetings, however, if your prospect wants a longer meeting, or wants to extend the meeting, great! The goal in sharing these strategies with you is to increase your prospects willingness to meet with you.

9.4 DOES A COLD "DROP-IN" MEETING STILL WORK?

Something I get asked regularly when I'm delivering my Unstoppable Sales^SM Prospecting Program is, "does dropping in to see a cold prospect still work"? The assumption by many sales professionals seems to be that this strategy is out of date and no longer effective. They provide reasons to support their theory, including a growing number of companies that don't have someone sitting in reception, increased security limiting access to anyone beyond the front gate, and prospects working from home. All relevant, but does that reduce the effectiveness of cold drop-ins?

I'm here to tell you that dropping in cold to meet a prospect can still be effective, particularly if face-to-face meetings are an effective means of selling your product or service. In fact, if your territory is broad (i.e., you cover the US Northeast), drop-ins can be more effective to get in front of a prospect as compared to other strategies like cold phone calls, cold emails, or social messaging. Let's begin then by addressing why the concerns, although somewhat accurate, don't justify removing cold drop-ins from your list of prospecting activities.

Myths About Cold Drop-ins:

Myth #1: Increased Company Security Makes Drop-in Meetings Impossible: There is some truth to the fact that some companies have put a greater protocol into place for security, much of which was prompted during the pandemic to control visitors; however, in my experience and that of many of those I train, most of these protocols are no longer followed. For example, there may be a restriction on visitors who don't have appointments; however, this doesn't stop you from attempting to connect with your prospect. More on how to make such attempt and some options for language in just a moment.

Myth #2: Prospects Work from Home so Drop-in Meetings Don't Work: It's true, there are an increased number of people who work from home since 2020; however, since this time, most companies have requested, or even demanded, employees return to the office at least part-time. Numerous studies have shown that there is a growing expectation of CEOs that their employees return to work, and additional studies have shown even younger generations are seeking employment where in-office experiences exist.[27] Additionally, if you are selling to a position that is at the executive level, they almost always spend at least some days each week in their office.

Myth #3: Stopping by Unannounced Upsets Most Prospects: This reason is one that is often not based on fact but rather opinion. Possibly you've had the experience of stopping by to visit a prospect unannounced, and either they don't come to see you in person (i.e., "Sorry, John's in a meeting right now and can't meet with you."), or you've had the experience of a prospect telling you they don't appreciate or accept "drop-ins." The latter is rare, but it can happen (ask me how I know). The reality is, any instances where a prospect may not appreciate your drop-in, or agree to meet with you despite being available, are far fewer than you might think. Most prospects will give you time if you stop by to see them, recognizing you invested time and effort (and possibly traveled a distance) to do so.

There are some criteria to consider when confirming if including cold drop-ins in your prospecting process will be a good strategy for you, as follows:

1. Your product or service is a high-dollar value item.
2. Your prospects are in a focused geographic area that you can reach with relative ease.
3. Your best prospect conversions happen because of in-person discussions.
4. Competitors use mainly virtual methods (i.e., email and video) to connect with prospects.
5. You sell a highly complex or technical product or service.
6. Drop-ins are convenient for you, given your proximity to your prospects.

If at least some of these criteria align with your circumstance, then using cold drop-ins as part of your initial prospect outreach is something you should be practicing. The next logical question then becomes how to position the drop-in for the greatest impact. Fortunately, there are several different, yet highly effective drop-in strategies you can include in your prospecting process. Below I'll describe each, as well as when they are best used, and how to ensure each is effective.

9.5 COLD DROP-IN STRATEGIES FOR GREATEST IMPACT

1. **The "In Your Area" Strategy**: In this strategy you reach out to a prospect proactively, identifying a date and time in which you'll be near their office or facility, suggesting you drop-in to introduce yourself. In this strategy, the prospect is likely to not have met you or only met you briefly (i.e., at an event). The prospect must also clearly understand what you are selling, and you need to provide a compelling reason for them to want to meet you. Examples of reasons to meet might include a referral (i.e., "Bob suggested I stop by to introduce myself") or a follow-up to a previous brief meeting (i.e., "I'll be near your office and wondered if you had a few minutes to meet. I have a report to drop off that I mentioned in my earlier message").

2. **The "Something to Drop-off" Strategy**: The difference between this strategy and the "In Your Area" strategy is that the latter is a proactive strategy often organized weeks in advance. Consider it a planned "cold stop-in" in which you provide the prospect with little notice, if any. This strategy is best used when you can offer prospects a sample, test product, or some other tangible information that they would find useful or helpful.

3. **The "I Was Driving By" Strategy**: In this strategy there is no notice to the prospect at all. You simply walk in and either ask reception to meet with the prospect, or you use the phone to dial the prospects extension (if there is no reception). To increase the likelihood the prospect will meet with you, and to convince reception (if they exist) to contact the prospect on your behalf, it is good if you can have something of relevance to give them. When asked, you can say something to the effect of "I had some information to share with Susan that is somewhat confidential" or "I have a sample I wanted to give to Joe, but it requires a brief explanation."

4. **The "Wanted to See Your Facility" Strategy**: Similar to the "I Was Driving By" strategy, when you use this strategy, there is nothing to provide the prospect, but rather your objective is to see the facility, which might include a large office, processing facility, or manufacturing facility. If what you sell is something that would be physically delivered or integrated into the facility (i.e., photocopiers, technology, and equipment), or if the use of your services requires an assessment of some kind (i.e., landscaping, HVAC), this can be a highly effective strategy.

5. **The "Just Wanted to Introduce Myself" Strategy**: This last strategy is similar to "Wanted to See Your Facility"; however, it is best used when you sell a service or something more personalized in nature, whereby a face-to-face meeting is often an expected or welcomed part of the process. Some examples of who might use this strategy include Lawyers, Accountants, Benefits providers, etc.

As mentioned earlier in this chapter, Depending on what you sell, in-person meetings may or may not make sense. The general rule I like to apply is, the higher the value of the product or service you sell, the more likely you should use in-person meetings to build a trusted relationship and improve your chances of converting the sale. This isn't always the case, but it is a good rule of thumb that tends to apply most of the time.

For your cold drop-in checklist and to boost your confidence for every drop-in you make, visit www.unstoppablesalesprospecting.com.

Now that we've discussed when and how to incorporate cold drop-ins into your prospecting process, let's talk about how to use networking to generate and warm-up leads in your prospect pipeline.

UNSTOPPABLE SALES PROSPECTING SYSTEM ACTION STEP

How are you using in-person meetings to improve your prospecting results? Can you adjust your method or approach to improve their effectiveness? Which of the cold drop-in strategies could you try that you haven't already?

10

The New Era of Networking

There are two different perspectives on networking as a prospecting strategy. Some use networking as a key part of their strategy and have great success; then there are those who have attempted networking, had little to no success, and, as a result, avoided it.

To start with the obvious, networking, that is, strategically socializing with others who can connect you with selling opportunities, is often more challenging for those who view themselves as introverted versus those who are extroverts. However, the idea that "networking is for extroverts" is a story that introverts tell themselves to escape the often-uncomfortable environment that networking can create. Being in a large and crowded room, introducing yourself to strangers, and attempting to strike up or carry on conversations with people you know little to nothing about makes most introverts uncomfortable.

Let me share some good news. Networking for leads doesn't have to be a random activity designed to make your life uncomfortable. I know dozens and dozens of introverts who use networking to generate the majority of their leads and are happy doing so. No panic attacks, no discomfort.

If you use networking as part of your primary prospecting strategy, you'll enjoy this chapter (if you don't, you may reconsider your decision). We'll uncover a system for you to use to ensure your networking efforts result in qualified leads eager to meet with you. Alternatively, suppose networking isn't something you are using today to generate leads, or it's not something you are comfortable with. In that case, we'll dispel any myths about networking and give you a system that ensures you don't have to wander around aimlessly at events saying "hi" to uninterested strangers.

DOI: 10.4324/9781003604457-13

10.1 NETWORKING AS PART OF YOUR PROSPECTING STRATEGY

Whether you are comfortable with networking or not, it can be a great way to build your list of qualified prospects and develop referral sources who can, in turn, introduce you to more qualified prospects! When done well, networking can take considerable time, but the benefits of building your pipeline can be dramatic.

When done correctly (to generate an unstoppable flow of new qualified prospects), networking consists of activities before, during, and after the event. In other words, for each event you intend to network at, there are activities you'll need to execute before you arrive at the event, once you're at the event, and after you return from the event. The latter is the most crucial step.

Before we get to the steps of your networking system, let's define what constitutes an ideal meeting for you to apply these steps.

Select Your Ideal Prospect Networking Meetings:

1. Carefully identify specific events you can attend and that your ideal prospects (i.e., decision-makers) will also attend.
2. The events you choose should offer you the opportunity to meet and interact with your ideal prospects while at the event (i.e., there is networking time in the schedule). Events that fill the day with speakers, lecturers, or breakout sessions with little to no time planned for networking aren't always the best option, as it will be difficult for you to execute your networking strategy.
3. Events you choose do not require you to become a sponsor or include any rules that limit your ability to approach or engage with ideal prospects (Note: this is rare, but I have seen events that frown on allowing suppliers or vendors to participate in the event other than as a trade show participant).
4. The events you select are situated in locations where you can organize in-person meetings outside of the venue. For example, local coffee shops, restaurants, or sports bars can be used to organize meetings with prospects.
5. Be careful about selecting events that offer attendees the chance to bring their spouses. Often, prospects select these events as a "vacation" with

their spouse. As a result, it can be difficult to convince them to spend time with you, as they will be dedicating any downtime to their spouse or partner. The exception to this rule is if your ideal prospects are small business owners, in which having their spouse present might be beneficial, as many small business owners make decisions that include their spouse or partner.

Bonus Tip: If the event allows you to access attendee lists (from previous events) or registrants for the event you plan to attend, this is a bonus, as it will lessen the work in your pre-event step.

With your optimum networking events now selected, let's dive into the steps for you to take to execute your Unstoppable Sales^{SM} Networking System:

Stage 1: Pre-Networking Steps – Your Goal: Arrange meetings while at the event. Commence six to eight weeks before the event, taking the following steps:

1. **Develop a list of event attendees**: Look for past attendee lists (often posted on event websites) or seek access to the list of current registrants. Capture this information in our event outreach list. Note: Ask the events coordinator for this information *before you register*, allowing you to assess whether the prospects you seek will be at the event before you pay to register.

2. **Search for past attendees**: Visit event pages from previous years and social media posts from past events (LinkedIn is great for this) to identify who has attended in the past. Capture this information on your outreach list.

3. **Develop your outreach script**: Draft a script you'll use to reach out to prospects, asking about their attendance at the event, asking a provocative question, sharing something of value, and then suggesting a brief five-minute meeting (Note: In subsequent chapters, we'll discuss this script, which is similar across all forms of outreach and not limited to just attending events).

4. **Reach out to prospects using various relevant channels**: Commence outreach, set a weekly target, and use appropriate channels such as LinkedIn, email, direct mail, etc. This outreach aims to arrange a brief meeting with your prospect while at the event. Continue following up (when prospects don't respond) until the event date. Be prepared at the event to search for those prospects you didn't hear back from.

5. **Suggest meeting options and timing**: Prospects may initially not want to meet with you at the event, so suggest brief meetings (e.g., 15 minutes) and interesting locations. For example, "Would you have five minutes to grab a coffee and discuss ___" or "I noticed there is a Starbucks on-site; if you have a few minutes, I'm happy to provide a copy of ____." Note: Many prospects will want to meet off-site, so make sure you find locations at the venue where you can meet but avoid being interrupted.

6. **Book off-site meetings where necessary**: Where prospects agree to meet, ensure you book a meeting spot to avoid the embarrassment of getting there and not having a seat. It is difficult for a place like Starbucks, but it is easier when you use a restaurant or sports bar.

7. Create a schedule for all your meetings that guides how you'll spend your time at the event. This way, you'll know when to seek out new prospects and what time is committed to existing meetings.

Stage 2: Networking at the Event – Your Goal: Connect with Ideal Prospects and Have Meaningful Conversations

Your time at the event should be consumed with seeking out, meeting with, and speaking with prospects. In other words, your success at finding and connecting with prospects at events in the available time is determined by your ability to have a well-executed plan. Many sales professionals attending events or trade shows have no real intention other than "to meet people." The problem is, even if you are effective at approaching and engaging with strangers at events, there is often no way to tell who your ideal prospects are amid the crowd. Furthermore, having a meaningful conversation with a prospect that isn't arranged in advance is typically near impossible.

With your pre-booked meeting schedule in hand, you'll know before the event what times are available for you to seek out prospects to engage with while at the event and what times you'll be tied up. Here are the steps you'll take once on-site at the event.

1. Identify open blocks of time and plan who you want to meet with. Begin by looking at your original outreach list. Who did you presume was in attendance but didn't hear back from or you couldn't organize a meeting with? These are the people you'll pursue during unscheduled downtime.

2. Prioritize the targets you wanted to connect with (and with whom you reached out) in order of importance. For example, if you reached out

to a CEO (a decision-maker) at Company A and a COO (a decision-influencer) at Company B, place the CEO at the top of your list.

3. Identify where you might find these people. For example, you can ask at the event sign-in if they've registered or arrived, visit their company booth if there is a trade show, or spend time at any gathering area, keeping your eye out for them. Note: You can use LinkedIn or other online tools to identify what your prospects may look like, which will help you validate who they are when you see them. Photos you find online might be outdated, but they give you a starting point.

4. Fill the unused time with random networking. If you've found and spoken with the ideal prospects you originally intended to meet at the event, spend the remaining open time in your calendar connecting with other ideal prospects with whom you may not have been aware.

5. Find referral partners for your power circle. You will meet others who sell a noncompetitive product or service to your ideal prospect at these events. Get to know these people and build relationships. Where you find multiple connections in noncompeting industries, suggest a follow-up call and explore options for sharing referrals. When you can make a team of referral sources from noncompeting sectors, I call this your power circle, and they can be a fresh source of new leads, introductions, and referrals.

Stage 3: Post-Networking – Your Goal: Arrange follow-up meetings to continue conversations.

Once the event is complete, the real work begins. Armed with business cards and notes from your meetings, now the real work – your follow-up – begins. Additionally, you'll want to follow up with those you had intended to connect with but couldn't (i.e., they weren't at the event, or you didn't get a chance to meet). Begin your follow-up immediately upon return from the event with your goal of completing the first round within two weeks of the event. The steps for your follow-up are as follows:

1. Prioritize all the connections and leads from the event:
   - Ideal prospects (decision-makers and influencers) with whom you met.
   - Ideal prospects with whom you didn't meet (but were at the event).
   - Ideal prospects whom you reached out to but didn't meet (weren't at the event).

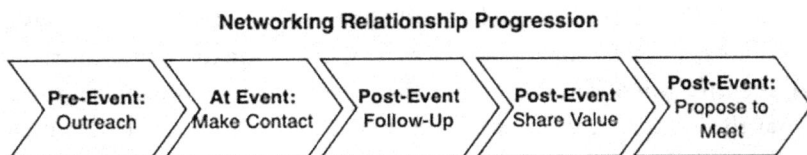

Networking Relationship Progression

| Pre-Event: Outreach | At Event: Make Contact | Post-Event Follow-Up | Post-Event Share Value | Post-Event: Propose to Meet |

DIAGRAM 10.1
Networking Relationship Progression.

2. Each group's goal is to continue the conversation but with some distinctions depending on whether you had a conversation. For example:
   - **Prospects you met**: Reach out to share anything promised and suggest the following steps.
   - **Prospects you didn't meet**: Reach out to share something of interest from the event and suggest a brief meeting.
   - **Prospects who didn't attend**: Reach out to share something you learned at the event (that's relevant) and suggest a brief meeting.
   - **Connections for your power circle**: Reach out and suggest a further conversation to explore referral opportunities a month or two out (giving you both time to follow up with prospects first).

As you will note from the steps described above, the goal of networking is to make connections that lead to meetings while at the event rather than just showing up and hoping for the best. Diagram 10.1 shows how this works.

With the steps in your networking process set, let's discuss a strategy that will save you time and, most importantly, make it easier to connect with and arrange future meetings with those you meet while at an event.

10.2 NEVER TAKE BUSINESS CARDS: DO THIS INSTEAD

If you've ever attended a networking event, one of the most common activities you'll find taking place is the exchange of business cards (although this is happening less as younger generations prefer to use technology for tracking connections). I haven't owned business cards in nearly a decade, but it's not because I have a website (www.shawncasemore.com) or a LinkedIn profile to point prospects toward. The reason? Instead of asking for their card or offering mine, I mentioned that I didn't have any business cards, so I pulled out my phone and asked for their email address or phone number.

For example, if a prospect asks you for your business card, you might say: "Unfortunately, I'm all out of cards, Julia; what's the best email address to use, or would you prefer text?" Then, you pull out your phone and prepare to enter their information on the spot. Alternatively, if the prospect you meet has shown interest in some information you discussed, you can say: "John, happy to send that report over we discussed; what is the best email to send it to?"

If you haven't used this strategy, you'll be surprised at how many prospects will stand there and spell out their email or phone number (for texting) as you type.

Bonus Tip: If both you and the person you are meeting carry an iPhone or Apple Watch, you can hold the display of your iPhone or watch an inch or two from the top of theirs. A Namedrop interface will appear on both screens, allowing you to share your contact information without the laborious task of typing in emails or numbers. Additionally, you will then have ALL their contact information!

When networking, your goal is to get a direct line of contact to anyone (relevant) you meet at the event. Asking for a business card or sharing yours positions you as the same as every other sales professional, and as I've shared previously in this book, Same Doesn't Sell!

Suppose the event you are attending is massive in size, with hundreds or thousands of people, and you can't connect with all the individuals you'd like. In that case, you can grab their business card (a common practice at significant events with an exhibit area or trade show). Then take what you can get. Just use an app like Vision-e or Covve to scan the cards. Alternatively, if you use CRM software such as Hubspot, Salesforce, or Zoho, you'll find that they provide apps or features for scanning business cards and uploading them into your CRM.

Before we leave the topic of business cards, let me share another best practice for you. For every new person you meet, you must take notes to remember what you discussed and your next steps. Although I've never been a big fan of business cards, one of the benefits they can provide is white space to take notes. For example, when I was selling in my twenties, if I met someone and received their business card, I would write a note on the back – something personalized and the following steps to take. This way, when I returned to my desk, I knew what to do with everyone I connected with.

Of course, for anyone who gives you their business card, you can still apply this practice. You can take notes on your phone for those who don't receive a business card. However, standing in a corner typing notes or writing notes on a business card is not the best use of your time (and you likely look odd to everyone else in the room). What you can do instead is text yourself a note about the person. In doing so, if someone approaches you and asks what you are doing, you can say you're sending a quick text. If you don't want to use SMS texting, you can send yourself a WhatsApp or email, or if your CRM software contains an app, you can type directly into CRM notes on your phone. Whatever method you choose, capturing notes will ensure you know what to do as a next step when you return to the office, which will save you time and help you get to your follow-ups even faster.

10.3 THE GOAL AND STRUCTURE OF EFFECTIVE NETWORKING

After our in-depth discussion on networking, the question that may remain is where your networking fits into your overall Unstoppable Sales^SM Prospecting System. The answer to this question depends on the degree to which you can find and connect with your ideal prospects while networking. There are three key questions to explore to assess if networking will be a good fit for your prospecting:

1. Are there associations that your prospects belong to and that hold regular in-person meetings?
2. Do these events allow me to participate and network? For example, contractors' associations often hold monthly meetings; however, they don't allow outside suppliers or vendors to participate. Alternatively, if you sell your product or service into various sectors, specific sectors offer dozens of event opportunities for you to engage in. For example, there are numerous events for healthcare providers to choose from, but fewer for lawyers, if that's your ideal prospect.
3. Is networking at these events an acceptable practice? Many events contain education sessions or speakers, with little time to speak with prospects except for lunchtime. These can still be effective; however, it's more difficult as no dedicated time is available to network.

Beyond these high-level considerations, there are some rules to assess whether networking is an effective strategy to include in your prospecting.

10.4 SHAWN'S EIGHT RULES FOR PROSPECT NETWORKING

1 Chose events that your ideal prospects participate in
2 Ensure decision-makers attend the events
3 Events include time for networking and interaction
4 You can access and participate in these events (as a supplier or vendor)
5 Your ideal prospects are willing to meet or engage at these events
6 You have budget available to support travel to the events
7 You use a system (like that described above) to connect with prospects
8 You place a strong focus and effort on pre- and post-networking activities

If networking allows you to find and connect with your ideal prospects, then you should include it in your Unstoppable Sales[SM] Prospecting System. Regardless of what you sell, nothing matches the power of personal connection for building trusted relationships, and it's through these relationships that you'll differentiate yourself, your company, and your offer.

In Part Four, we will begin combining all these ingredients into one simple system you can use to elevate your prospecting game to unstoppable levels.

UNSTOPPABLE SALES PROSPECTING SYSTEM ACTION STEP

What improvements should you make to your LinkedIn profile? How can you become more active to demonstrate your credibility? How will you incorporate LinkedIn messaging as part of your outreach strategy?

Part Four

Prospecting Mastery
Indirect Methods to
Connect with Prospects

To this point, we've discussed various methods, including email, LinkedIn, and even direct mail, as effective means of placing yourself in front of your ideal prospects. Doing so should differentiate you from your competition and earn the attention of your prospect.

I'm confident, however, that several of you are wondering whether there is a less intrusive way to connect with a prospect – a method that doesn't involve cold outreach and that can warm a prospect up or even attract them to you. Good news! There are several methods to warm up cold prospects, and in this section of the book, we'll cover the three most important for you to include in your Unstoppable Sales^{SM} Prospecting System.

As we dive into indirect methods to connect with prospects, you'll find some strategies you already know, whereas others may be foreign or something you haven't attempted. My advice is to read Part Four in its entirety, and only after doing so should you consider which strategies you want to introduce or

DOI: 10.4324/9781003604457-14

improve upon. In other words, don't jump over this section and dismiss it because it contains practices or methods you are already using. There are all sorts of best practices, tips, and nuances within each method that I can promise you are different or, at minimum, can enhance what you are practicing today.

So, sit back, grab a notepad or your laptop, and let's explore some more advanced strategies for warming up prospects and attracting them to you!

11

Build a Tsunami of Referrals

According to a study conducted by the Brevet Group, 91% of customers say they'd give referrals.[28] However, only 11% of sales professionals ask for a referral. In other words, most of your customers, or those who have had a positive experience working with you and your company, would be willing to provide you with a referral.

If you are like many of the sales professionals I meet, your approach to soliciting referrals from your clients or customers falls into one of three categories:

1. You've never asked for a referral and expect that customers or clients who appreciate you and the work that you do will automatically give you one if the opportunity presents itself.
2. You have asked for referrals in the past but rarely receive one. Therefore, you only ask when your customer or client gives you or your company a compliment (and you remember that it would be a great time to ask for a referral).
3. You use referrals as a key part of your prospecting strategy, repeatedly asking every client for introductions to others in their network.

Whatever category you fall into, referrals can be one of the easiest, most effortless ways to connect with your ideal prospects. So much so that I know many sales professionals that all they do is solicit referrals, and they generate so many leads they don't need to practice much else.

That said, this level of success often requires you to spend sufficient time in your existing role to develop a list of satisfied clients or customers. You also require steps to solicit referrals (multiple times) throughout your sales process. If you do not have the latter, let's begin by discussing a method to gain access to new and eager-to-buy prospects.

DOI: 10.4324/9781003604457-15

11.1 USE REFERRALS TO GAIN ACCESS TO PROSPECTS

Let's begin with the most apparent reason you might not receive enough referrals. If not done correctly, most referral requests lead to a "let me think about it" response. The prospect may want to help, but how they can help isn't apparent. For example, asking a vague question, such as: "Do you know someone who might be interested in our services?" will ultimately result in a vague answer, like "yes." The reality is that every single prospect and customer you've ever interacted with knows someone you could sell to (read that twice).

Any request you make will likely fall flat without a specific description of who you seek, their title, role, responsibilities, company type, or geographic region. Here's a better question: "Susan, are there other CFOs you know within the Chicago area who might also use a service similar to ours?" Presuming she says yes, you'd follow up with "Great! I'm looking to connect with CFOs who work in insurance brokerages like yours (noncompeting, of course) in the Chicago area. Who are the top three you'd recommend I reach out to?"

Specificity is the key to soliciting referrals. However, you'll also notice that the ask contains questions that dig deeper to uncover the referral. You aim to build a dialogue rather than an interrogation and educate your prospect or client on whom you seek to work with. Like peeling back an onion, the deeper we go with our referral asks, the more opportunities we'll uncover. Let me give you some examples:

Example #1: Susan responds to your original question above with, "I'm new to the Chicago area, so I don't really know any other CFOs in the area." If your territory expanded beyond the Chicago area, or you wanted to pass along a referral to a co-worker who handled a different region, you might follow up with, "Interesting; where did you live before?"

Example #2: Susan responds, "I'm the president of our Chicago CFO group," to which you reply, "Interesting. Do you ever bring in outside speakers to your monthly event?" (presuming you are comfortable giving a presentation), or "Are you looking for sponsors for the group?"

Suppose Susan shuts you down, providing you with very closed-ended responses. How might you dig deeper without becoming annoying? In this instance, transition to a more open-ended and vague question to cast a broader net in hopes of igniting other ideas. Let's look at an example of how this might play out.

Example #3: Susan responds with a simple "no," which you might follow up with, "Would you like to connect with other like-minded CFOs in the area? I'd be happy to connect you with some of my clients, and I believe there is even a Chicago CFO group." In this instance, you've attempted to add value before you follow up with the ask. Now, suppose Susan responds with "No, thank you." In this instance, you can ask your question and clarify why it's essential, for example: "Understand Susan. The reason I ask is that most of my clients are referrals from other clients I've worked with. It's how I make a living. I was just curious if there were others in the insurance industry in the area you might suggest I reach out to."

One quick mention. Did you notice I snuck the word "prospect" into that example? I did so because creating a tsunami of referrals happens when you expand your "ask" beyond just customers or clients and begin approaching everyone whom you believe could offer a referral. That includes prospects, past clients, colleagues, lost prospects, etc.

11.2 SOCIAL MEDIA STRATEGY: FIND REFERRAL INTRODUCTIONS

Earlier, we discussed using LinkedIn[29] as part of your outreach strategy (when prospects are present). LinkedIn also offers you a powerful tool for identifying referral opportunities. There are two different methods you can use to do this.

Option 1: This is a free option if you have an active profile on LinkedIn. From your LinkedIn profile, you can search for a connection, and when you select their profile, directly under their number of "Followers," you will see small icons (of the profile pictures of your mutual connections) and next to this, a link with the names of mutual connections. Select this link, and it will take you to a page that lists the profiles of your mutual connections (at least at the time of this writing you can).

Option 2: This is a paid option you can get if you invest in LinkedIn's Sales Navigator,[30] which costs around $100 per month as of this writing.

While logged into Sales Navigator, find and select a prospect profile. Once you do, a section will display their connections, including any mutual connections you share with them. Another option, if you have co-workers who also use Sales Navigator (Enterprise version) is to select the "TeamLink" feature, which allows you to identify potential prospects and connections through your team members' connections within Sales Navigator.

Whether you have a free version of LinkedIn or a paid version, the platform offers you a simple way to identify mutual connections for referral opportunities. Before we discuss how this works, you might think, "But Shawn, this only shows me mutual connections, so a referral to a prospect isn't possible as I already know these people." That would only be true if you were not using LinkedIn as part of your outreach. Your Unstoppable Sales^{SM} Prospecting System encourages you to use LinkedIn as part of your initial outreach to prospects you don't know but would like to connect with. As a result, your network will consist of people you don't know or don't know well.

It's also important to mention that decision-makers who don't know you will connect with you on LinkedIn. As referenced in the earlier chapter, my studies have found that if your LinkedIn profile and the content you share are relevant and valuable, then approximately 40% of cold prospects will accept a connection request with no personalized invitation. Just send the invite. The only restriction is that you can only send invites to second-level connections (at the time of this writing). I'll discuss this further in a future chapter, but for now, consider that if you are reaching out cold to connect with second-level connections, your LinkedIn network will contain many potential prospects with whom you'd like an introduction, which in turn will show you even more "mutual connections."

11.3 STEPS TO OBTAIN A REFERRAL ON LINKEDIN

Now that we've discussed how to use LinkedIn as part of your referral system, let's discuss the steps you should take to obtain a referral. There are two methods to do so, as follows:

Method #1: Obtain a Referral to Connect Outside LinkedIn

1. Identify a prospect within your LinkedIn network (who has accepted your connection request) and with whom you'd like to get a personalized introduction.

2. Using the steps above, identify who else in your network (that you know reasonably well) is also connected with this person.
3. Reach out to your contact (identified in step #2 above) with a direct message on LinkedIn like the following: "Hi John. I noticed we have a mutual connection with Bob Smith, and I wanted to contact him. Do you have his contact information?" Send a follow-up message in two weeks if you don't hear back.
4. If your referral source, in this example, "John," says they don't know "Bob Smith" or aren't sure how you know "Bob" is a mutual connection, simply mention that you noticed through LinkedIn connections that he is a mutual acquaintance and wants to reconnect with him.
5. If your referral source provides you with "Bob's" contact information, you can then reach out to Bob (using this information) and mention who provided you the information, in this instance, "John."

Method #2: Obtain a Referral to Connect within LinkedIn

1. Identify a prospect within your LinkedIn network (who has accepted your connection request) and with whom you'd like to get a personalized introduction.
2. Using the steps above, identify who else in your network (that you know reasonably well) is also connected with this person.
3. Reach out to your contact (identified in step #2 above) with a direct message on LinkedIn like the following: "Hi John. I noticed we have a mutual connection with Bob Smith, and I wanted to contact him. Have you spoken with him recently?" Send a follow-up message in two weeks if you don't hear back.
4. If your referral source, in this example, "John," says they don't know "Bob Smith" or aren't sure how you know "Bob" is a mutual connection, simply mention that you noticed through LinkedIn connections that he is a mutual acquaintance and wants to reconnect with him.
5. If your referral source responds and identifies that they know Bob but haven't spoken in several years, thank them and let them know you'll mention his or her name when you reach out.
6. If your referral source responds and says they don't know Bob and aren't sure how they are connected, then attempt to find another mutual connection and begin the process again.

7. Finally, send a message through LinkedIn to Bob. Mention your mutual acquaintance early in the discussion (e.g., "Hi Bob, I was speaking with John recently, whom I believe you know"), and then use language like what's been mentioned already in this chapter.

With these strategies in mind, let's discuss building momentum in generating a tsunami of referrals by considering everyone you interact with as a referral source.

11.4 EVERYONE IS YOUR REFERRAL SOURCE

As you'll have noticed in this chapter, there may be several reasons why you may not be receiving a referral. Even an ecstatic customer or client, faced with a specific request for a referral that doesn't require much of their time to produce (i.e., you make it easy for them by simply asking for an email introduction), may decide not to move forward if any of the following exist:

1. They are busy and referring others to you is a low priority.
2. They aren't immediately clear on who they could introduce you to.
3. They must figure out what to say if they introduce you.
4. They need to figure out when the right time is to make an introduction.
5. They need to see an immediate personal benefit to making the introduction.

When you realize the many obstacles keeping your customers or clients from providing you with referrals, it's easy to understand why you aren't repeatedly obtaining them. Let's shift the question from "why" you are not receiving referrals to "how" you can obtain more referrals given these obstacles. What are the steps to take to ensure that all your satisfied customers or clients are eager and willing to make introductions to others?

There are eight steps to put into practice, which form the foundation of continuously bringing a tsunami of referrals to you.

11.5 SHAWN'S EIGHT RULES FOR UNSTOPPABLE REFERRALS

1. You mention the desire for a referral during the discovery dialogue with every prospect.
2. Ideal referral candidates are clearly defined (i.e., type of company, title, position).
3. Referral asks are predetermined and planned for each customer or client's journey.
4. Measures are in place to track when referral asks take place.
5. A referral request is made for every lost sale (pending the relationship remains intact).
6. Every lost customer or client is asked for a referral (pending a solid relationship).
7. Existing customers or clients are asked for a referral every six months at a minimum.
8. Other customer- or client-facing employees are skilled and confident in helping you solicit referrals (more on this in a moment!).

It's easy to see how adding these steps will significantly increase your chance of obtaining referrals. However, I recognize that they might seem a bit overwhelming or possibly too difficult to introduce all at once. If this is the case for you, start by introducing one at a time.

For example, you could begin with step 7 above and, once this is in hand, add step 6.

However, you chose to implement these eight steps. Ensure that the referral ask isn't a burden for your client or customer, but rather, you make it easy for them to say yes and make the introduction. For example, you can suggest that you reach out (with your customer's permission) and mention your client's suggestion that you call. You could also ask if there is someone they'd like to invite to an upcoming lunch or an event you might be having with your client.

Next, let's take the idea of referrals from prospects, customers, and lost customers to the next level by strategically building a referral partner network in Chapter 12!

UNSTOPPABLE SALES PROSPECTING SYSTEM ACTION STEP

How often are you asking for referrals? Can you improve your scripting, your language, and the frequency with which you ask to increase the chances of gaining referrals? At what points will you ask, and of whom? Track your results!

12

Develop a Power Partner Network

What if you could have an army of credible business professionals who know you, like you, and trust you, mentioning your name and making introductions to your ideal prospects on a daily, if not weekly, basis? How would this impact your ability to increase your pipeline, generate more opportunities, and convert more business? Substantial.

That's the power of developing your Power Partner Network: a hand-selected group of business professionals who sell noncompeting products or services to your ideal prospects and with whom you build a mutually beneficial business relationship.

Building a professional network that can give and receive referrals is not a new concept; however, it is a more common strategy in some sectors than others. For example, the insurance, financial services, and banking sectors rely heavily on building networks of professionals willing to give and receive referrals. If they succeed with this strategy, so can you!

For the strategy to succeed, you need to identify who sells to your ideal prospects and their companies and then make a concerted effort to connect with them. Let's explore the steps to developing your Power Partner Network.

12.1 BUILDING YOUR POWER PARTNER NETWORK

Your Power Partner Network, or PPN, is a group of business professionals who sell products or services to your ideal prospects. Examples of the kinds of roles these professionals might exist in can vary depending on what you sell, so here are some broad examples:

- Lawyers (who provide legal services to your ideal prospects and their companies)
- Recruiters (or those who help your ideal prospects find new jobs)
- Accountants (or those who sell accounting services)
- Software or hardware providers (i.e., those who sell SaaS or cybersecurity)
- Manufacturing agents (if you sell a manufactured product)

Once you've identified those who may be good candidates for your PPN, the following steps are to determine how to best connect with these individuals. You can reach out to them directly to connect; however, it's often a more straightforward approach to identify events you'll attend and where these individuals may attend. Here are the three most common methods of connecting with potential referral sources:

1. **Events**: Take time while at events to find and connect with prospects and observe who else is attempting to do the same thing. Introduce yourself and make connections you can follow up with afterward to explore a relationship.
2. **Trade shows**: When attending trade shows (or events with a trade shows) to prospect, look at who has a booth at the show to identify potential referral partners. Please don't spend too much time here speaking with them at these events; instead, introduce yourself briefly and suggest a coffee or conversation after the event.
3. **Direct outreach**: When you obtain the contact information of someone who might be a good candidate for your PPN, you can contact them directly. Send an email or give them a call, explaining who you are and what you sell and suggesting a brief conversation to see if there are any ways you can help each other out.
4. **Referrals from your PPN**: As you begin to find and engage with referral sources, you can ask who they know, who might also sell to your ideal prospects, and who might be interested in joining your PPN.
5. **Clients**: You can ask clients who they work with, who sell noncompetitive products, and whom they suggest you connect with to share ideas and networks. You'd be surprised how many clients are happy to share potential referral partners. Additionally, since clients know you, your style, and your personality, they often share someone with a good connection.

12.2 A STORY FROM THE SALES FLOOR

I've spoken for CEO executive groups such as Vistage, TEC (The Executive Committee), MacKay CEO Forums, and Innovators Alliance. After presenting at one of the events, a gentleman approached me and introduced himself. He was a new executive chair who had heard my talk and wanted to ask if I'd be available to come and speak with his group.

I did, and he invited me back several times, periodically asking for my help to fill a last-minute spot where a speaker had canceled. We became friends, talking on the phone periodically, and one day, he reached out and asked if he could introduce me to a member of his CEO group who needed assistance with their sales. The unexpected referral turned into a two-year coaching engagement with a client where I coached their sales team to improve conversion rates. He introduced me to several more prospects, and we became friends over the coming years. I, in turn, connected him with some in my network who were potential members of his CEO group.

The relationship formed naturally; however, this was when I first realized the true power of a PPN. After that, I began working intently on building a network of professionals with whom we could mutually share introductions.

Unfortunately, my friend passed away several years ago. Although I couldn't attend his celebration of life due to a previous client commitment, many of our mutual acquaintances and clients told me that hundreds of CEOs and executives were in attendance. He had built a robust network of professionals who supported his business growth and whom he supported in return.

Your PPN can be formal or informal, meaning you can officially make it known that your goal in the relationship is to share referrals back and forth openly. Alternatively, you can focus on building a relationship in which you are both clear about the value each of you brings to your clients but never formally discuss exchanging referrals. I prefer the former, which doesn't mean you can't become close friends. Still, it's essential to make your initial intentions known – that the value of having a mutual relationship is sharing business referrals.

You should also structure your PPN to use your time best. Rather than having random calls with each member of your PPN, you can bring them together to meet once the group reaches a size of six to eight people. I've seen sales professionals do this formally, such as inviting the group for dinner or a social outing every quarter. At the same time, others prefer to hold virtual meetings to bring their PPNs together. This latter approach is typically due to the distance between each PPN and the difficulty in bringing them together.

Your PPN can extend beyond other business professionals who sell to your ideal prospects and should include your existing clients or customers.

12.3 CAPITALIZING ON CUSTOMER RELATIONSHIPS

You have a long list of customers or clients you've worked with, in both your current and previous roles. Even if you are new to a company, there is a network of past customers or clients who have grown to know and trust you and the company. These can be a gold mine of referrals waiting for you to tap into them. However, before you do, let's be clear on exactly how to mine this source of referrals best.

12.4 SHAWN'S STEPS TO MINE CUSTOMER RELATIONSHIPS FOR REFERRALS

1. Identify existing customers with whom you've worked and have a good relationship.
2. Identify past customers (from previous roles) with whom you've worked and have a good relationship.
3. Combine these lists and then prioritize based on the strength of the relationship (the top of the list is the strongest, and the bottom of the list is the weakest).
4. Develop your outreach script, which should include a request for a "brief chat to get their opinion on something you're working on." Ideally, this should take 15 minutes.
5. Begin by reaching out to connect. Start with a call and leave a voice message that mentions your desire to connect. Then, less than a week later, send a follow-up email.
6. Have your discussion (whichever channel makes the most sense) and make notes to schedule your following outreach. Depending on the size of your network, the frequency is every 6–12 months.

Note: This process differs from asking your customers or clients for a referral, which you should have set up as part of your sales process and which I discuss at length in my book *The Sales Multiplier Formula*. Instead, reach out to past customers or clients in your current and previous roles to reconnect and ask for a referral.

When mining past customers or clients for referrals, keep the discussions conversational. Your goal is to rekindle your relationship genuinely, and while doing so, mention who your ideal prospect is (be prepared to describe them entirely), and then ask who they might suggest you reach out to that fits this description. For the most part, you'll find these conversations enjoyable (these are people you already have a relationship with) and an easy way to solicit referrals.

When your past customers or clients become a part of your PPN, you drastically increase the frequency and quality of the referrals you gain. In other words, you put past trusted relationships to work, helping you generate more business and referrals.

If soliciting referrals from past clients or customers sounds like an easy target, let me share another one that might not be so obvious: your prospects.

12.5 USING NEW PROSPECTS TO FIND OTHER PROSPECTS

When I work with sales teams, training them on various processes to fill their pipeline with prospects, I'm always surprised at how few use their existing prospects for generating referrals. The most common concern is not wanting to irritate or offend a prospect you haven't sold anything to, primarily for fear of losing the opportunity to sell to them moving forward.

These concerns are valid, but what's most important about this process is the timing during which you solicit the referral. Diagram 12.1 identifies the ideal time to ask for a referral from an existing prospect.

There are three points in any prospect relationship in which asking for a referral makes sense (to the prospect) and at which you have the best opportunity at receiving the referral.

Referral Ask #1: *The Indirect Pre-Proposal Ask*

Make this request before you issue a proposal or quotation. By this point, you've built some trust and had an in-depth discovery dialogue (so you

Multi-Referral Request Strategy

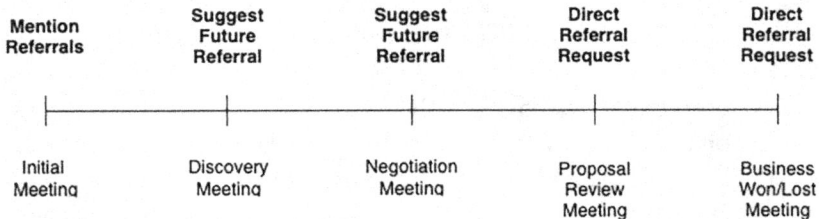

Mention Referrals	Suggest Future Referral	Suggest Future Referral	Direct Referral Request	Direct Referral Request
Initial Meeting	Discovery Meeting	Negotiation Meeting	Proposal Review Meeting	Business Won/Lost Meeting

DIAGRAM 12.1
Multi-Referral Request Strategy.

understand more about your prospect), and the question is less direct than at other points. Here are some examples:

"John, before I send you a proposal, may I ask a question?" (John responds with a yes.) "Now that you know more about me, our company, and the value our product/service can provide, is there someone you know in a similar role that you suggest I want to reach out to?"

OR

"Stefanie, before I send over the quote we discussed, may I ask a quick question?" (Stefanie answers with a yes.) "I'm always looking to connect with other CFOs like yourself, and I'm curious if there is someone in your network with whom you think it would make sense I reach out and connect."

Referral Ask #2: The Proposal Acceptance Ask

The second ask, which can be grouped with the first or done on its own, is done when a proposal by a prospect is accepted. In other words, it's at the point of conversion from prospect to customer that you ask about a referral. Here are some sample scripts to demonstrate:

Hi Joe, I've been looking forward to our working together and appreciate your trust in both myself and our products/services. Since you know quite a bit about us at this point, I was wondering if there is someone in your network of peers, another general manager, who you think we might also be able to assist.

OR

> *Samantha, I am excited to work with you and your team on this important project. Since you are familiar with our company, our solutions, and our team, I was curious if there is someone you know, either within your company or in your network of peers, who is in a similar role and who might also appreciate the value we can provide. Would you be willing to make an introduction?*

Referral Ask #3: *The Proposal Rejected Ask*

This last option is the one that most sales professionals push back on. For many, asking for a referral, which can seem like a favor, may seem wrong after a prospect has rejected your quote or proposal. However, it's a great time to ask. Suppose you've done everything right (i.e., been responsive, provided value to your prospect, built a trusted relationship, and put a solid proposal or quote forward). Your prospect will likely feel guilty when they tell you, "Sorry, we're going with someone else." Presuming you did everything right and made a good impression, there's no reason they wouldn't follow through and give you a referral if you ask. Here is some example language:

> *Francesca, I'm sorry we won't be working together at this time, and I'm hopeful there will be an opportunity to explore this again. In the meantime, considering you now know me, our team, and the solutions we provide, would there be someone in your network of peers, at the VP or director level, who you would suggest I speak with?*

OR

> *John, I'm disappointed we won't have the chance to work together right now. However, I was wondering if I might ask a favor. You know how I assist companies like yours, and I was wondering if there is someone in your network who you'd recommend I connect with.*

You can see, by these varying examples and scripts, that there are a multitude of points at which you can ask a client or a prospect for a referral. When you do so, knowing you've put your best foot forward to build trust with the other person, and with the conviction that a referral is something they can easily provide to return the favor, you'll find yourself surrounded by referral partners, who won't just refer one person but will continue to make introductions over time. The key is to build a robust network of referral sources, your PPN, who can repeatedly make introductions to those you can sell to.

UNSTOPPABLE SALES PROSPECTING SYSTEM ACTION STEP

How often do you ask for referrals? Assess the best times to include an ask in your process. Do you have a Power Partner Network? If not, who might you pursue that would be interested in sharing referrals? Can you start asking lost opportunities for a referral?

13

Associations

Spend Time Where Your Prospects Gather

Associations have long offered an opportunity to connect with prospects. However, the problem is that many sales professionals don't put the necessary effort into seeing results. Like any other form of prospecting, using associations to connect with prospects and build relationships takes time and effort. Additionally, for association prospecting to be effective, you must build relationships with those who run the association, contributing to their priorities and offering support where possible. Associations do not appreciate salespeople who (they believe) bother members and do not contribute to the association, making it challenging to build meaningful connections.

Fortunately, there are many ways to connect with prospects through associations, with varying degrees of effort and time required for their effectiveness. This chapter will discuss common ways to prospect using associations and the effort and timelines needed to experience a consistent stream of new prospects fully.

13.1 FIND AND JOIN ASSOCIATIONS TO CONNECT WITH PROSPECTS

To begin with, you should identify those associations in which your ideal prospects spend time. You can use many resources to identify these associations, including a quick Google search. Or there are resources such as my colleague Sam Richter's IntelNgin,[31] which can help narrow your search results and allow you multiple ways to search for associations and association contacts, doing much of the grunt work for you.

DOI: 10.4324/9781003604457-17

Use the following criteria to determine whether an association is a good fit for your prospecting purposes:

1. What associations serve or support the sector you are trying to sell to?
2. Is the association focused on bringing members together for learning and sharing? (i.e., some associations only provide lobbying for their members and are not a good place to try to connect with potential members.)
3. Does the association have events or trade shows you could attend or participate in? If they do not, it will be difficult for you to make and build meaningful connections.
4. Does the association allow members who aren't directly in the industry? Some associations restrict members or participants to those who work in the industry and will not allow those outside the industry to get involved.
5. Are there local or regional chapters? When there are smaller groups outside the leading association, such as regional chapters, your ability to connect with those who operate and support the association will be much easier than at a national level.
6. Are your competitors involved in the association? Are there articles published by your competitors, ads displayed on the association website, or are they featured as a sponsor? If so, you may think you shouldn't get involved; however, the reality is quite the opposite. If your competitors are involved already, it demonstrates that you should get involved, as there are opportunities.

Once you've worked through these criteria, you should have a list of associations to consider joining or getting involved in, but don't jump into signing up quite yet. Attending association events, particularly if it requires travel, can be costly. Additionally, your time is valuable, so we want to be selective about which ones we belong to.

To prioritize the most relevant associations to your prospecting, use the chart in Diagram 13.1.

Your goal through this exercise is to shortlist associations to a minimum of three and a maximum of five so that you can determine which would be the most beneficial for you to get involved in. There are five steps to assess each association for its relevance and value to you. Due to the size and various methods to engage with associations, your assessment could take a few weeks or a year to complete.

Association Criteria Scoring	
1	Support/Serve My Score: Score of 0–5_____
2	Networking Opportunities: Score of 0–5_____
3	Event and/or Trade Shows: Score of 0–5_____
4	Ease of Accessibility: Score of 0–5_____
5	Local or Regional Chapters: Score of 0–5_____
6	Competitive Landcape: Score of 0–5_____

DIAGRAM 13.1

Association Criteria Scoring.

13.2 SHAWN'S FIVE STEPS TO ASSESS ASSOCIATION VALUE FOR PROSPECTING

1. **Identify an Event to Attend as an Observer**: Select a premier or marquee event, as these are most likely well attended. Set aside time to participate in the event and interact with other members, identify who is in attendance, how willing they are to connect, etc. Note: If the event offers a chance to be a sponsor or exhibitor, avoid doing so at this point. You aim to attend an event to observe whether the association (and the event) might offer you a good opportunity to find and connect with prospects.

2. **Conduct Preliminary Association Prospect Research**: Not every association or event will benefit your prospecting purposes. For this reason, research before your chosen event to assess who might be attending. Some options to do this include visiting event webpages to see who was in attendance last year and searching for event hashtags on social platforms like LinkedIn to view information from past events. You can also contact the association directly, ask to speak with someone in the membership department, and tell them you are considering joining the association and planning to attend this event to assess whether it would be a good idea. If asked, be forthright about your intentions; however, mention your desire to "get more involved to support the sector and network" rather than suggest that your main goal is to find prospects. There is a reason why you'll share this as your primary purpose, which will become evident in the following few rules.

3. **Connect with Decision-Makers While at the Event**: During the event, take every opportunity to meet with and speak to attendees to assess who the prospective customers and key decision-makers are. If there are formal networking sessions, attend them and make it your goal to connect with as many people as possible to fully determine the number of ideal prospects (for you) in attendance. If a trade show or hall exists, walk the floor to assess who is exhibiting. Are your competitors there? If so, it's a good sign that the association offers opportunities to connect with prospects.

4. **Connect with Association Staff While at the Event**: Your goal while at the event is to meet association staff, as they offer you a direct line to many of the members, can give you an idea of how to best meet and connect with your ideal prospects, and can offer you opportunities to get more involved in the association on a committee or board, which will help you build further relationships. Make mention you are considering membership and ask about whether your ideal prospects typically attend events, how many events they get involved with, and any other information that would be helpful to assess the value of the association for prospecting purposes. Note: Avoid getting involved with the association early (i.e., in the first 12 months). Some associations are desperate for volunteers and will load you up with various committees and activities before you can fully assess if the association is a good source of prospects.

5. **Investigate Options to Become Known**: If the association, through your research, consists of many of your ideal prospects and appears to offer many opportunities to connect with your ideal prospects at various events and other functions, then look for ways to become known. For example, if you enjoy presenting, does the associate look for presenters or speakers at their events (online or in person)? Does the association offer in-kind opportunities to sponsor events (i.e., they provide a sponsorship opportunity in return for something you do for the association, such as a special program or offer for their members)? Every association seeks subject matter experts to speak, host, facilitate, or even write articles. If you have the expertise to share that allows you, your company, your products, or your services to become known, then explore what makes sense and dive in!

Now that you have thoroughly vetted some associations to join and connect with your ideal prospects, let's discuss using association events specifically to generate leads on an ongoing basis.

13.3 USE ASSOCIATION EVENTS TO
FILL YOUR CALENDAR

If, through your research above, you've identified several associations where your ideal prospects spend their time, then you have an opportunity. In most instances, these ideal prospects won't be begging to buy from you. Remember, your competitors also attempt to connect with these prospects, so your approach must be very strategic. Why? Have you ever attended a networking event only to overhear someone trying to sell to someone else? I have, and let me tell you, it's painful to listen to, and despite the salesperson's best intentions, it can result in a perception of desperation. Your goal is to be perceived as a trusted advisor, not desperate.

To achieve this recognition level and ensure prospects are drawn to you (rather than repelled by you), you need a process to follow that allows you to meet with prospects, one-to-one, during these events. You read this correctly: you will meet with prospects at these events in a structured fashion, and they will want to meet with you rather than be repelled by your desperate attempts to try and sell them.

When it comes to generating business from association events and meetings, there are ten steps you should apply for every event you attend. I refer to this as Shawn's Association Event Prospecting Method, and it consists of three different stages, as follows.

13.4 SHAWN'S ASSOCIATION EVENT
PROSPECTING MODEL

This method aims to build trusted relationships with prospects by becoming someone they find interesting and insightful; someone prospects seek to get to know.

Pre-Event Activities: This stage begins six to eight weeks before the event and consists of some research and initial outreach. Your goal is to identify who will be attending the event and arrange a brief meeting with them. Authors Note: This strategy works best after you have attended the event one time to vet its potential for prospects, further to my suggestions above.

Step 1: Identify who might be attending the upcoming event. You can search for lists of attendees (some events will share these with you once you register to attend), review previous websites and social posts to learn who has attended, or review member lists on association websites. Where all else fails, create a list of companies you believe could be (or should be) a member.

Step 2: Reach out to inquire whether the prospects are attending and suggest a brief meeting. Keep this outreach personalized and focus on adding value rather than pitching or presenting. For example: "Hi John, we met last year at the ABC event in Brisbane. Wondering if you are planning on attending again this year?" OR "Hello Susan, hope you are keeping well. Are you planning on attending the ABC event again this year? There was something I was hoping to get your perspective on, which should only take a few minutes."

Step 3: Book brief informal meetings with those who respond. For each person who responds positively (i.e., attends), suggest a short discussion at a predetermined meeting place. These can include the lobby or lounge areas of the event space, a local coffee shop, or an area that event organizers have set aside for meetings.

Step 4: Send something of value to confirm your meeting. For those who respond positively to your request to meet, send them something of value that confirms the meeting. At the very least, this could be a short email the week before the event, such as "Hi John, looking forward to meeting next Tuesday at 10 am. Coffee is on me!" A better strategy, however, is to share something that the prospect will find useful or helpful in some way. "Hi John, in advance of our connecting next Tuesday, wanted to share this study I came across for your industry. Have you seen this? Looking forward to connecting!"

Event-Centric Activities: Presuming your efforts to generate meetings have been successful, your calendar should have several pre-arranged meetings planned at various times during the event. As you build relationships, these meetings will increase, filling your calendar. Any time with no meetings booked should be spent attempting to find and connect with prospects you don't know but would like to meet with at future events. In other words, network among those in attendance to find others with whom you can connect and then arrange meetings in the future.

Step 5: Attend all Pre-Scheduled Meetings: Ensure you have time scheduled to attend the meetings you've planned and leave buffer time between (i.e., 30 minutes) where possible to allow yourself the chance to make notes, capture next steps or follow-up steps, and prepare for upcoming meetings.

Step 6: Meeting Structure and Objectives: For each meeting you hold, there are two main objectives. First, you must get to know the individual you're meeting with more personally. What can you learn about their needs regarding your products or services? Although these may seem like obvious goals, getting sidetracked and doing one of two things is easy: either you avoid getting to know the person individually and jump right to business or spend most of your time discussing business and not getting to know the individual personally. The key is to balance the time you have. Of course, if your prospect drives the conversation and jumps right to business, you should follow suit, but I've found that by having these two objectives for each conversation, most sales professionals balance their time well.

Step 7: Set Objectives for Connections during Downtime: Before you attend the event, you should have a good idea of how much downtime you'll have. Based on this, you should prioritize your time in two ways: first, connecting with those likely to be in attendance but who did not respond to your outreach. Second, connect with those you haven't met with previously who represent your ideal prospects for future meetings.

Post-Event Activities: This is where the real work begins. Once you return from the event, you must reach out to everyone you initially reached out to within the first two weeks. This includes everyone you attempted to book a meeting with while at the event but who didn't respond, everyone you did meet with, and everyone new whom you connected with.

Step 8: Complete all Follow-up and Next Steps from the Event. For example, is there information you need to send, resources to follow up with, or additional meetings to book? Once these are completed, follow up with any new connections from the event again to share information, insights, etc.

Step 9: Follow Up with Those You Didn't Meet with or Who Didn't Attend: Based on those who didn't attend or whom you didn't see at the event but whom you have originally reached out to, reach out to share observations and insights from the event. Your goal here is to continue sharing value and building the relationship so they will be willing to meet at a future event.

Step 10: Identify Improvements to Your Process: Based on your pre-event planning and time spent at the event, what improvements should you make? For example, is more time required between meetings or less? Should you arrive a day before to hold more meetings? Is there value in scheduling time to walk the exhibit floor and connect with exhibitors who might represent future participants in your Power Referral Network?

Following this ten-step approach, you will gain significant leads and new opportunities from every event you attend. When done correctly, it is a lot of work, but if your ideal prospects attend events, they can be your primary source of new leads.

Become known as someone who regularly attends events. Association employees will take notice and eventually approach you to determine if you'd like to get more involved in the association. Before jumping on the bandwagon, let's discuss the opportunities and how to use them for prospecting purposes.

13.5 ASSOCIATION INVOLVEMENT: GET CLOSER TO YOUR IDEAL PROSPECTS

Suppose you've identified some associations with events that contain your ideal prospects, and the events have allowed you to meet and connect with prospects. In that case, you should dive into the association even deeper. Most associations seek volunteers to support the association in various capacities, including committee members, volunteers, and board members. These can offer you ways to get more involved and gain increased visibility to members of the association, for example:

Volunteers are often used to assist with events, helping to check in members and introducing session speakers.

Committee members can speak with members directly and, in some instances, are also used during events as hosts, session facilitators, etc. Depending on the association and its structure, there are various committees to consider joining, so be sure to investigate those committees that include member involvement, such as an "Event Committee" or "New Membership Committee." By participating in a committee, you will have the opportunity to connect with other members and build relationships.

Board member positions come with stature and can bring more awareness to members of yourself, your position on the board, where you work, etc. Board members are often drawn upon to speak at events, introduce speakers, and even hand out membership awards. Additionally, you'll have the chance to get to know other board members, building closer relationships than if you approached them at an event.

Before you run out and sign up to support the associations where you may find your ideal prospects, let me clarify something essential when using association involvement as a prospecting strategy. These positions all require time and effort, so you will often need to give up your time. For example, board meetings can be on weekends or evenings; committee meetings are common and frequent, often happening during the day or in the evenings, and outside of these meetings, you will be assigned actions to complete and things to bring back to the next meeting. The duration and frequency of meetings and the amount of effort and time you'll need to invest can depend on the association; some are very demanding, whereas others take very little time.

So, although association involvement can be a great way to gain exposure, become known by members, and build closer relationships with other members than is typically possible, it will require you to commit your time to it.

Additionally, in any of these positions, remember that you can't rush trusted relationships, and you don't want to be the person who volunteers to join a committee or board and then attempts to pitch everyone there. You'll need to put in work and time to become known within the association, so this strategy can be what I refer to as a "long burn." In other words, building awareness and relationships that lead to new business generation can take years. However, if the association is ripe with ideal prospects, it may be well worth your time and effort.

UNSTOPPABLE SALES PROSPECTING SYSTEM ACTION STEP

What associations do your ideal prospects participate in? Can you arrange some events to attend to vet if joining would make sense? Is there an association you are already involved in, and which has yielded leads, that you could get more involved in?

14

Speak to Sell

Become an Authority

Did you know that 77% of people have some level of fear of public speaking?[32] As a prospecting method, this next strategy may not be for everyone.

Speaking to sell is one of the best ways to become recognized as an authority in your field. Additionally, it is one of the only ways you, as a sales professional, can put yourself in front of a room of prospects and have their undivided attention, presuming you do a good job and don't bore them to tears. In other words, speaking on a specific topic, related to what you sell and presuming you are good at doing so can result in many prospects approaching you to connect, to learn more about what it is you sell, and in some instances, even to inquire about having a meeting with you or buying what you sell.

As someone who speaks professionally for a living, I can tell you that the fear of speaking in public is something you can get past if you have the desire to do so, and like any other skill, the harder you work to improve your craft, the more effective you will be. When I began speaking professionally in 2009, my presentations were not all that great – reading notes from a podium with a monotone voice, repeatedly saying "ah" or "um" while pointing to PowerPoint slides that were overcrowded with content, making for a very underwhelming presentation! To keep improving my skills, I will observe other professional speakers at the top of their game and introduce changes in my approach, demeanor, and content. Today, I speak at sales kickoff events and association meetings globally numerous times each month, and this is the primary way I generate leads for my sales training, coaching, and advisory work. In other words, speaking to sell is my primary strategy, and one

DOI: 10.4324/9781003604457-18

I have shown hundreds of sales professionals to use themselves, regardless of what they sell.

Are you curious whether speaking to sell is a good strategy for you? Let's start by discussing how to transform your presentations in the boardroom and online into prospect conversion machines.

14.1 CONVERT YOUR SALES PRESENTATIONS TO SELLING MACHINES

In this section, we'll discuss three ubiquitous presentations that, as a sales professional or business development professional, you are likely already practicing in the early part of your prospect interactions (hint: if you aren't, you should be), as follows:

1. **Prospect Introductory Presentation**: Also referred to as a standardized or canned presentation, this is the introductory presentation you might make once you've met a prospect. The intention is to familiarize them with your product or service and your company. These presentations can be delivered virtually or in person.

2. **Needs Satisfaction Presentation**: This is a presentation often used after the Discovery Dialogue, with the intention of showing how your product or service will satisfy each prospect's needs that they've shared in the earlier discussions. They are often delivered before or immediately following a proposal or quotation, allowing the prospect to learn more about how you will address their needs and ask questions to clarify your offer or proposal further. These are sometimes commonly used as part of an official RFP process but can also be asked of potential vendors or suppliers to clarify their recommendations further.

3. **Product Demonstration Presentations**: These are commonly used for technical products or software or for an experiential interaction with a prospect to influence their decisions. Demos can be delivered live, prerecorded, or in a hybrid version that contains a combination. Product demonstrations aim to demonstrate to prospective customers how a product works, allowing them to see firsthand the benefits they can achieve by using the product and recognize the ease with which they can use it.

Although these presentations differ in format and style, they all attempt to influence the prospect to want to buy your product or service and engage with you and your company. For our purposes, we'll focus on this area, specifically how to increase the influence and persuasion of your presentations.

Although there are many nuances to creating more effective presentations, which I cover in my Presentation Skills Mastery for Sales Professionals program, I'll share the most important and often overlooked strategies here. Keep in mind that I've generalized these, so you'll have to assess how best to introduce them into your own sales presentations.

Methods to Increase Sales Presentation Effectiveness – Your Behaviors

1. Always Maintain Eye Contact
2. Listen More than You Speak
3. Smile!
4. Engage Your Audience
5. Ask Provocative Questions

If you've ever watched someone speak, you'll know the impact of each of these five areas on the ability of the speaker to be influential and persuasive. Let's turn then to the not-so-obvious tips for presentation effectiveness. You do not need a slide deck to present to your prospect. Your goal in any presentation is to engage your prospects in a dialogue, and although images can be a powerful way to do so, they aren't necessary. If you deem a slide deck necessary, follow these tips to ensure they are engaging and not overwhelming (or overwhelmingly tedious!).

14.2 METHODS TO CONVERT YOUR SALES PRESENTATION TO A SELLING MACHINE – CONTENT

1. **Your Slides Should Start with a Question**: To engage your prospect immediately, once the pleasantries are out of the way, ask a simple question such as "Before we get started, may I ask, what were you hoping to discuss today?" The response then becomes your priority in how you proceed with the presentation.

2. **Use More Images and Less Text**: Presentations that are heavy with text are not engaging and distract your prospect from engaging with you – as they are too busy reading the slides. Instead, include more relevant images, such as pictures of your products, clients, facilities, customers' facilities, awards, etc. Pictures allow you to tell a compelling story to your prospects, so long as the stories are relevant, which will be more engaging. They also allow you to customize what you say to the prospect position without changing the presentation.

3. **Fewer Slides for In-Person; More Slides for Virtual**: During an in-person presentation, the number of slides for a 60-minute meeting can range from 5 to 20 (maximum), allowing time for discussion, questions, etc. During a virtual presentation, you'll need to work harder to keep your prospect's attention as they'll be in front of a computer dealing with incoming emails, tasks, reminders, etc. Target to have 15–30 slides for a virtual meeting, and while you present, make sure you flip between your slides and back to portrait mode (where you are only looking at the participants, not the slides) to engage your prospect. In this instance, you will need to increase the number of slides due to the frequent changes.

4. **Tips for Adding Videos, Sound, or Other Tech into Your Slides**: In my experience, it's always risky to add outside resources to your slides, such as videos, sound, etc. In a virtual environment, you have control over the Internet, links, etc., whereas in a personal environment, you do not. Speaking from experience, when I deliver an in-person experience, I rarely include outside links and resources; there is always a risk they won't work.

5. **Your Slides Should End with This**: End your slide presentation with an engaging question to explore how your product or service would impact the prospect. For example, "Susan, now that we've discussed how our service would improve your customer churn rates, what are your thoughts on the specific impacts to the bottom line?" or "Susan, it seems from our discussion today our service could have a significant impact on reducing your customer churn rates, what are your thoughts?" In these examples, you'll notice two things. One, I refer to the presentation as a "discussion," and two, I ask for their thoughts or perspectives. View your presentation as the start of a conversation rather than the end.

By applying these strategies, your presentations will have a greater influence on prospects for several reasons. First, they will be more focused on the prospect and their needs. Second, you will engage them in a conversation, which will assist in building trust and allow you to learn more about their needs, their company, and them as individuals. Lastly, your presentations will set you apart from the competition, who are likely still droning on and using the same boring presentations that you once did.

There are dozens of additional nuances, tips, and strategies to improve your sales presentation skills. If you'd like more information on mastering presentation skills as a sales professional, visit my website at www.shawncasemore.com or my YouTube channel at https://www.youtube.com/@ShawnCasemore.

14.3 SPEAK AT EVENTS TO BECOME A SUBJECT MATTER EXPERT

What if your ambitions to speak extend beyond presentations to your prospective customers? Do you want to become known in your sector or area of expertise, build a recognizable name for yourself throughout the industry, and be seen as a sought-after expert? If so, then you'll need to master one-to-many selling, which refers to speaking from a stage or in front of a large group of people, simultaneously, most of whom represent your ideal prospects, and to build trust and attract prospects to want to speak with you.

Speaking from the stage and selling one-to-many is different from delivering presentations in several ways, for example:

- Audience size (ranging from 50 to several hundred people)
- Audience composition (i.e., different experiences, knowledge)
- Slide content and application
- Increased sharing of stories and examples

Speaking from the stage is less about your content and more about the journey you take the audience on. Your goal is still to engage the audience; however, you do so through various stories and examples that are relevant to the audience. Additionally, your goal for speaking from the stage differs from presenting to prospective clients in an office setting. The primary goal of any stage presentation is to be viewed by the audience as an expert who understands their environment and challenges and has experience in resolving their most significant problems. Referred to as "stage presence," when done correctly, you will have several participants in the audience approach you after your talk to ask you questions and engage with you either at the venue you are speaking at or afterward by reaching out through email or social media.

Suppose you aren't getting these inquiries and questions after your talk. In that case, it's a sign that your presentation isn't interesting enough or capturing the interest of your audience. To reverse this trend and improve your stage presence, observe others who speak in your area of expertise and identify what they are doing differently that is effective at capturing their audience's attention. Be careful doing this, however, as your goal is to observe and identify methods to improve your speaking, so do not inadvertently take their content and make it yours!

Aside from this, a few other considerations in one-to-many speaking from a stage will ensure you generate inquiries and new leads.

14.4 SHAWN'S FIVE STRATEGIES FOR GENERATING LEADS FROM THE STAGE

1. **Give a Unique Perspective**: The best way to ensure your audience wants to engage with you after you speak is by sharing a unique perspective on something that is or will be a challenge for them to overcome. Paint a picture in the eyes of your audience of how your unique solution, approach, method, position, or product will address this common issue or future challenge they will face. For example, when I speak to an audience at an association event or in a Sales Kickoff Meeting, I share new ways to sell B2B and demonstrate, through various client examples, how these approaches are far more effective than traditional "feet on the street" approaches to selling. Being known for this differentiates me from other sales speakers who share outdated information and creates interest in my work, leading to inquiries after I've spoken. What common challenges do your prospects face, and what makes your product or service unique in resolving, overcoming, or addressing those challenges?

2. **Share Valuable Resources**: Throughout your presentation, mention different resources to help your audience address the common challenge, issue, or future struggle they face. Examples include offering a copy of your slides, a free assessment, a checklist, relevant books, a free sample, a trial period, etc. However, whatever you offer should be a no-strings-attached offer. Your goal is to add value and assist your audience with addressing their challenge or issue without holding them ransom to hire you or buy your product.

3. **Suggest a Conversation**: Depending on what you sell, it might make sense to offer a follow-up, in-depth, one-to-one conversation. Doing so can provide you with the opportunity to convert a prospect. The key is to mention during your talk, after you've shared a relevant client example, the chance for a one-to-one conversation about the audience's unique needs. Again, suggest this conversation with no strings attached and genuinely attempt to help the prospective customer during the conversation. This approach can be compelling when the talk you share is complex, and it gives attendees a chance to discuss their unique situation with you (although the situation may not be that unique to you) and test-drive the relationship with you.

4. **Identify the Next Step**: Like making an offer of a conversation, one powerful way to ensure follow-up conversations with prospective customers from the audience is to suggest outright that the next step for them is to book a meeting with you. If you've done a good job at sharing a unique perspective, your audience will likely be left wondering how your points apply to them and what the next logical step they might take is. Answer this question for them by suggesting a conversation at the end of your talk! Be explicit in your suggestion; however, make it a no-obligation discussion once again. For example, you might say, "If what we've discussed here today has been helpful, the next step would be to book a meeting with me or our team, where we will help you customize a specific solution for you."

5. **Make a Closing Offer**: Like the strategy above, a good strategy to engage your audience is to make an offer at the end of your presentation. However, the offer would be for something of value, not a conversation. The key to making the offer is to be highly appealing to them and present it with a sense of urgency. The urgency might include a "limited-time offer," a special discount code, or a free download. To ensure these are effective, make it the last thing you share in your presentation. For

example, "Before I leave you today, my team and I have put together something to assist you with addressing this important issue. Visit our booth in the exhibit area, and we'll provide you with a (insert what they would value here). Thank you for your time!"

If you really want to increase your ability to generate leads from the stage, combine all the above strategies to create a flood of inquiries following your talk! A quick note, however, to be clear: Your goal is not to outright sell from the stage; instead, mention these offers, next steps, and resources as part of your conversation and in the most natural way possible.

A final point. Nothing trumps experience. As someone who has spoken professionally for over 15 years, the talks I delivered back in 2009 and 2010 from the stage were awkward. Speaking from a stage to generate leads is part art and part science; it will take time and practice to get good. Put in the work, and you'll see the results!

14.5 FACILITATE DISCUSSIONS WITH CUSTOMERS TO ATTRACT MORE PROSPECTS

Another way you can speak to generate leads is by facilitating conversations with prospective customers or clients. Association events such as those we've identified above not only hire speakers but also hire individuals to facilitate "fireside talks," which are interviews of subject matter experts in the industry. You can also do this in an in-person or virtual environment and then capture and share the interview with others. You can earn credibility by attracting and interviewing interesting guests. When done correctly (i.e., using strategies similar to those shared above), it can attract prospects to you and your work. My podcast, The Sales Master's Roundtable, is a good example of this format. You'll find recent episodes on my YouTube channel, and you can search @ShawnCasemore[33] on YouTube.

Interviewing, and facilitating these kinds of discussions with existing or prospective customers, like speaking from the stage, is an art. Just watch the *Joe Rogan Experience*[34] or *The Howard Stern Show*,[35] where they interview guests as part of their show, and you'll see that holding a conversation that both engages the individuals you are interviewing and those who are observing or listening takes skill, talent, and a genuine interest in people.

Something that may not initially be obvious about this strategy is that as you gain momentum with your interviews (and interviewing skills), you'll attract others who want to be guests or would like to interview you. If you include the strategies mentioned above in Shawn's Five Strategies to Generate Leads from the Stage, you can actually begin converting interviewees into potential customers.

Lastly, like speaking, you can always make proactive suggestions to associations about individuals you would like to facilitate an interview with or offer up your customers if they are willing. Associations consistently seek fresh ideas and content, so this can be a great way to set yourself apart from those who speak and get a guaranteed spot on the event agenda.

UNSTOPPABLE SALES PROSPECTING SYSTEM ACTION STEP

What changes or improvements can you make to improve the impact and persuasiveness of your presentations? Are there other types of speaking to generate leads that you would like to try out? What is your starting point?

Part Five

Build Your Unstoppable Sales^{SM} Prospecting System

To this point we've discussed a wide variety of strategies you can use to prospect successfully, but now it's time to build your Unstoppable Sales^{SM} Prospecting system. The techniques or methods we've discussed to this point will seem like more work for you unless you build them into a system, something that you can repeatedly apply to achieve your desired results.

It's time to take action and transition from a sales professional who prospects to a sales professional with a highly effective prospecting system.

Let's go!

DOI: 10.4324/9781003604457-19

15

Multi-Channel Approach

Surround Your Prospect

We discussed earlier that it can take you between 8 and 16 touchpoints to connect with a prospect. The reality is, however, that it takes what it takes, meaning I've seen it take dozens and dozens of touchpoints over the years to connect with prospects. But how can you reach out to a prospect in a meaningful way through 8–16 touchpoints (or more!) without annoying them?

To begin with, you mustn't flog the same communication channel repeatedly. For example, sending 16 emails will position you as a spammer, not a sales professional. Sure, cutting and pasting emails all day may be productive, but with the increased inbox security and spam folders, email is an increasingly less effective way to reach your prospects. It's far better to use a multi-channel approach to reach out in different ways, with different content, and on various channels to make contact. It can take more up-front planning on your part and more time to execute; however, your chances of making a connection increase dramatically.

In this chapter, we'll discuss why a multi-channel approach is essential, what commonly effective channels to use, and how to build your multi-channel outreach method so that it is easy to execute.

"Haven't I Seen You Somewhere Before?"

When I started my sales consultancy 15 years ago (as of this writing), a mentor of mine continuously suggested I "put myself out there more often." My interpretation of this statement at the time was far different from what it is today, and it's something we can all learn from. To explain, in my business's early days, I needed people to begin recognizing who I was and the value I brought to the market. I needed to put my face, ideas, and experience

DOI: 10.4324/9781003604457-20

out there for people to take notice. Succeeding at prospecting requires you to consistently put your name, message, and value into the market. The main reason for this is something we mentioned earlier: that prospects today increasingly spend their time conducting research before engaging with sales. That shift in behavior has a significant impact on your ability to connect with prospects.

Let's look at an example I frequently run into when I work with a sales team. Suppose, for instance, someone reaches out to connect with you on LinkedIn, whom you don't recognize. What's the first thing you are likely to do? If you are like most people I know, you'll likely check out their LinkedIn profile; if you don't find them there, search their names on Google. Let's look at two very different scenarios that might occur.

In scenario one, the prospect finds your profile on LinkedIn, where it has up-to-date work experience (i.e., showing where you work, your role, how you help customers); there are numerous customer/client recommendations, recent posts, and shares of information that is highly relevant to your prospect, and the picture at the top of your profile is up to date with a professional photo. In scenario two, they find your profile on LinkedIn, but your image is either missing or noticeably dated; there is no recent content posted or shared, and your work experience is vague or outdated (worse yet, it doesn't have your current employer!). What are the chances a prospect will respond to your LinkedIn connection request in scenario one versus scenario two? As you might guess, scenario one has a far greater chance they'll engage with you.

What if they don't look at your profile on LinkedIn but instead look you up on Google, for example, possibly after receiving an email from you or meeting you at an event? From your experience, what link typically turns up on page one of Google when you search for your name or any name for that matter? Go ahead and search your name + your company name right now. I'll wait. Well, what did you find? If you are like most people who at least have a profile on LinkedIn, then a link to your profile will show up on page one (along with some other content that you might want to look further into!). Remember, your prospects are searching for you and your name, and what they find (regardless of its origin or location) informs them as to whether you are who you say you are and whether you sell what you suggest you sell.

To be clear, this is not a tutorial on using LinkedIn to sell, though there are resources on my website to assist you with this (www.shawncasemore.com), but rather to suggest that if you want to ensure prospects engage with you, it's important you consider what they find when they search for your name online, because, well, if you are reaching out and approaching prospects, they will look you up! By increasing and improving the influence of your presence online, you'll accomplish two things: first, prospects who look you up will immediately find your name and be influenced by what they see (which can immediately differentiate you from the competition); it also allows them a chance to get to know you and learn more about you, possibly by watching a video of you speaking at an event or reading a bit about your involvement in volunteer activities.

If you are not active on LinkedIn, you might want to reconsider your strategy. As the old saying goes, you need to spend your time where your prospects spend theirs, so if your prospects are on LinkedIn and somewhat active, then it's a place you should spend some time. Let me clarify, however, your goal is not just to be on LinkedIn but to be everywhere your prospects may look you up.

When you spend time in places your prospects spend their time, you create credibility and familiarity, which, when combined with your outreach, accelerates the prospect's knowledge of you and deems you as someone worth trusting and learning more about. Let's look at a scenario to demonstrate how this might come together. Suppose you've reached out to a prospect on LinkedIn to connect, and they recognize you immediately because:

- They met you at a recent event (i.e., you approached them at their booth and engaged in some interesting conversation).
- They recognize you from a panel discussion you participated in at your industry association event earlier in the year.
- They received a report by mail from you several months ago that identified key economic impacts on your industry. It had a personalized and signed note attached that simply stated, "Susan, I thought you'd find this report interesting."
- You invited them to a special event you organized for companies like theirs last year.

On top of this, when they Google your name, up pops your LinkedIn profile page, which is current and on which you are highly active, allowing them to find recent posts you've made about challenges in their industry, on which many of their peers have commented. To top it off, you've got dozens of mutual connections in common that show up on your LinkedIn profile, and they notice you commenting on posts from other sources in the industry (i.e., the association they belong to). Are they likely to accept your connection request? The answer is yes, 100%!

My point is this: You've got to place yourself strategically everywhere your prospects are and lay a foundation demonstrating that you are a recognized resource, expert, and/or peer in their industry. In other words, your goal when interacting with a prospect should be to have them respond to you by saying, "Don't I know you from somewhere?" Remember, prospects look you up; you don't know it. What will they find when they look you up on Google, Bing, or LinkedIn?

15.1 BALANCING PROSPECT OVERWHELM WITH PROSPECT INTEREST

As you likely know by now, I practice what I preach. My business, like yours, requires that I continuously prospect if I want to make new connections and generate new clients. Between my prospecting and the prospecting systems I help sales teams introduce, I've observed there are three key ingredients to ensuring you are effective when prospecting, namely:

1. **Your Mindset about Prospecting**: First, your goal in prospecting is not to sell but to make a meaningful connection with a prospect to assist, support, or help them. Sure, ultimately, you want to sell them your product or service, and you need to be clear on this to remain focused. However, your mindset must be that of wanting to connect to be useful.

2. **Be Consistently Consistent**: Being successful in prospecting requires consistency. To the extent that you are consistent, in other words, you are always focused on filling your funnel with new relationships and new opportunities. The highest-performing sales professionals I know have numbered targets set for how many people they will prospect weekly and monthly, and they hit those targets regardless of sick days or vacation days.

3. **Using Creativity as a Guide**: Not every prospect will connect at the same time, and even though you'll consistently work to adjust and improve your outreach and the value you provide, not every prospect

will engage at the same time, for obvious reasons (varying priorities, interests, at different points in their buying cycle, etc.). Creativity, exploring different languages and methods to connect with prospects, is key to your long-term success.

If you are to reach out to prospects using multiple channels, the obvious question is, won't all this outreach from me overwhelm or even annoy my prospects? The short answer is no if you follow some simple guidelines. Remember, the goal is to create an environment where our prospect begins to realize they've seen us before, and we pique their interest in wanting to engage.

15.2 SHAWN'S GUIDELINES TO AVOID PROSPECT OVERWHELM

1. **Accelerate Your Outreach Touchpoints**: Your goal is to ease your way into their world, not bust down the door and announce your arrival, so start your touchpoints a week apart, and then slowly reduce the duration. For example, touchpoint #1 is Day 1, touchpoint #2 is Day 8, touchpoint #3 is Day 14, touchpoint #4 is Day 19, etc. We discuss this strategy and its application in greater depth elsewhere in this book.
2. **Be Transparent in Your Touchpoints**: When you reach out on different channels, ensure that you reference your previous outreach. For example, you might send a LinkedIn message referencing an earlier email (e.g., "Hi Sara, I sent you an email last week, but I'm not sure it made it, so I thought this might be a better way to connect."). Being transparent builds trust and avoids coming off as a spammer.
3. **Vary Your Outreach Methods**: As mentioned previously, our goal isn't to annoy the prospect and jam their inbox or voicemail but to slowly earn their trust. Additionally, every prospect will have preferences for which channel you engage on, so try using various outreach methods. Using the example above, touchpoint #1 might be an email, touchpoint #2 might be a LinkedIn connection request, touchpoint #3 might be a voice message, touchpoint #4 might be a new email, etc.
4. **Focus on Adding Value and Being Helpful**: When you reach out to a prospect, you ask them to give you something they cherish more than

anything else in the world – their time. For that reason, you need to consider "giving" value (i.e., resources, tools, samples, trials, information, and studies), all of which help the prospect address their questions, challenges, and needs, and that gives them back time. By doing so, you create the perception that you are someone who can help them gain more time in their day, and as a result, they will be willing to give you their time.

5. **Be Responsive to Prospect Needs**: When a prospect does respond to your message, email, or connection request, be immediately responsive. Your goal is to demonstrate that you are there when they need you. Although this may be undesirable to hear for some of you, if a prospect responds at 8 pm (and you see the message), you should consider at least acknowledging their response. Keep in mind, we don't want to train a prospect to think we are always available; however, if they've found time to invest in you at 8 pm, then you might consider returning the favor.

But what if your prospect is annoyed by your various attempts to connect with them? Well, first off, if someone doesn't suggest that you are too assertive in your pursuit of connecting with them, you likely aren't trying hard enough. Remember, prospecting is about earning your prospect's attention, and some may view your various attempts and methods to connect as assertive, and that's okay. Even if you have a prospect who becomes annoyed with your consistent but varied attempts to connect, they at least now know and recognize you – which was your goal all along. Note: Your goal is not to annoy them; however, don't be too concerned if a prospect occasionally suggests such a thing. If it's not most of the prospects you pursue, you are doing just fine.

If this does happen, however, here is how I suggest you respond.

15.3 FIVE STEPS TO RESPONDING TO AN ANNOYED PROSPECT

1. Apologize, and suggest you were excited to connect with them and may have been overzealous (i.e., "My apologies Thom, I may have gotten overly excited to connect.").
2. Give them a compelling reason for why you wanted to connect that has nothing to do with selling them something (i.e., Our mutual

connection John suggested we should connect"; or "I wanted to connect with you before the ABC event next week.").

3. Ask if there is a better time to speak (i.e., "Would there be a better time to speak; how about next Tuesday morning or Wednesday afternoon?").

4. Slow down and focus on building a personalized relationship (i.e., "I'll be in your area next month, would you have a few minutes to meet in person?").

Now that we've discussed a balanced approach to communicating with your prospects and the need to create the impression that "they've seen you elsewhere," let's combine this into something you can easily deploy – your very own Unstoppable Sales^{SM} Prospecting Multi-Channel System.

15.4 YOUR UNSTOPPABLE SALES^{SM} PROSPECTING MULTI-CHANNEL SYSTEM

In this section, we will identify several different multi-channel communication systems that you use in your prospecting process. This isn't about what messages you send or the timing of sending them, but rather how to create a multi-channel communication strategy that will help you quickly and effectively earn the attention of your prospect.

There are three building blocks you'll need to consider building your system, namely:

1. Communication Methods – Consider the characteristics of your ideal prospect, how their role requires them to communicate, what their average day looks like, and what their preferred method of communication might be. If you aren't sure, ask an existing customer or client. If you don't have any (i.e., you are new to the role), reach out and ask to interview someone in the role to get a sense of their preferred communication methods.

Use the answers to these questions to determine the best communication methods to earn and retain the attention of your ideal prospects. In doing so, consider the following three questions:

• What medium would have the most significant impact on this relationship stage?

- What would be the best follow-up method for each message?
- What mediums are your competitors using, and how can you differentiate?

Let's look at an example:

You are contacting a VP of Operations to schedule a call or video meeting. This role is typically very busy, with days full of back-to-back meetings. In a multi-facility company, this role might spend considerable time traveling to other facilities. The personality of a VP of Ops is typically very direct – they don't want a ton of analysis or information but rather facts and relevant data. They always keep their smartphone with them and are inundated with emails and text messages.

2. Communication Mediums – Considering the information above, which channels are most relevant and effective for communicating with your ideal prospects? Consider the following list of examples, and select at least four (4) that you think are relevant:
   - Email
   - Online Forums
   - LinkedIn
   - LinkedIn Groups
   - Facebook
   - Facebook Groups
   - Instagram
   - Direct Mail
   - SMS text
   - WhatsApp
   - Webinars and Virtual Events
   - Telephone Calls

To continue with the VP of Operations example, you might conclude the following mediums make the most sense:

Initial Outreach – Personalized message on LinkedIn
2nd Outreach Message – Send direct mail with a personalized note
3rd Outreach Message – Call (intent of leaving a message) to see if your mail arrived
4th Outreach Message – Send a video message (via email)

You get the idea.

If you receive a response through any of these outreach channels, stay with the channel the prospect communicates on, as it is a sign that that is their preferred means of communication with you. For example, if your VP of Operations accepts your LinkedIn connection request, send a follow-up message to "thank them for connecting." Then, you might wait five days and send a second personalized LinkedIn message that asks them a relevant question.

3. Communication Message – The length, structure, and content of your messaging must capture the interest of your ideal prospect. There are many nuances to consider here, but let's discuss the most important using some rules to guide your message development.

Shawn's Rules for Effective Prospect Outreach Messages:

1. Personalize all messages to the prospect – name and circumstance
2. Initial outreach messages should be shorter in length – two sentences at most
3. End your initial messages with a question – your goal is to engage the prospect
4. Avoid sharing attachments and links in initial emails – they are spam red flags
5. Include personalized notes with any direct mail – make them colored to stand out
6. Be responsive when a prospect does reply – responsiveness demonstrates interest
7. Add value at every step – what is unique about your service, and how can it help?
8. Use three follow-ups for each missed response – don't overwhelm your prospect
9. After two months of no response – move to a quarterly prospect nurture program

With answers to the above questions and rules in mind, you now have a system for your multi-channel prospect outreach. In the next chapter, we'll discuss what a prospect nurture program is and how to introduce one.

To get a template to help you work through these system components, visit www.unstoppablesalesprospecting.com.

UNSTOPPABLE SALES PROSPECTING SYSTEM ACTION STEP

What new communication channels can you introduce that complement your other methods of communication? How will you use multichannel communication to create a perception for your prospect that you are "everywhere"?

16

Don't Lose Touch

Your Prospect Nurture System

One of the most common questions I get is, "How long do I pursue a prospect before I give up and move on?" I've encountered two different schools of thought on this topic.

The first perspective for pursuing a prospect is that you never give up. Your attempts to reach a prospect continue forever or for as long as you remember to pursue them! In this scenario, there is a lack of structure in the outreach, and attempts to reach prospects are varied and random. For example, someone using the "forever" approach might attempt to reconnect with a prospect each year at an event you both attend but doesn't make further attempts outside of the event.

The second most common response to this question is what I refer to as the "fixed duration" approach. The person prospecting sets several outreach attempts, and as you approach the maximum number, they begin to make it clear you will cease further attempts to connect with the prospect. These structured outreaches were made popular by online marketers who set a series of scripted and automated emails with an offer, often presenting something "for a limited time," to create fear that the prospective customer would miss out (otherwise known as FOMO). I've seen many sales and business development professionals take this same approach, most often to enable them to move on.

There is a problem with both methods. The first "never let them go" approach doesn't allow sufficient frequency of interaction to allow the prospect to truly get to know you or the value you provide. In other words, too much time between interactions with your prospect doesn't create curiosity

DOI: 10.4324/9781003604457-21

or interest in you or the value you bring. You won't be at the top of their mind if they need something you sell, and they won't see you as a trusted advisor.

The "fixed outreach attempt" method is often too aggressive. What's to say that after six emails, a prospect will suddenly want to speak with you? Sure, it might take only three emails and 15 varied interactions over 24 months. How will you know the correct number of interactions?

Each prospect you pursue is unique; they have their own experiences, interests, priorities, personality, preferred communication methods, etc. As a result, there is no way to know exactly how many touchpoints it will take to earn their attention. For this reason, your outreach should span upward of 16 different touchpoints, following which you then move them to a longer-term outreach strategy to continue to put your name and your ongoing value in front of them. The last thing you should do after investing time in pursuit of an ideal prospect is give up.

16.1 YOUR PROSPECT "KEEP IN TOUCH" STRATEGY

When it comes to keeping in touch with a prospect over an extended period, there are five questions you should address. Let's look at the following questions to formulate your keep-in-touch strategy:

1. When should you move a prospect to a longer-term keep-in-touch strategy (LTKTS)?

The answer to this question depends on several factors, including the uniqueness of what you sell, the frequency with which your prospect typically invests in your product or service, and your past experiences engaging with prospects. For example, you sell a highly complex product or service like technology that your prospect only invests in every ten years, and you've typically found it takes 12–24 months to close a new deal. Your initial outreach strategy is likely spread out over 12 months. As a result, you may move a prospect to your LTKTS between 16 and 24 months. If, on the other hand, you sell commercial insurance that a prospect invests in annually and you typically close a new deal in weeks, you might transition them to an LTKTS between six and eight weeks.

2. How often should you reach out to prospects in your long-term strategy?

As mentioned above, the frequency you reach out can depend on the complexity and duration of your typical closing cycle. If you sell a highly complex product or service with a 12–24-month closing duration, you might reach out once every six months. Alternatively, if you sell a commoditized product or service with a four-week closing ratio, your LTKTS might involve monthly touchpoints. I often recommend to the sales teams I work with that a quarterly reach-out is a good goal that allows you to plan the time it will take to put the outreach and value together.

3. What value should you provide that continues to build interest?

Your value should be like what you would provide while pursuing the prospect. Most importantly, it should be helpful to your prospects, keeping them updated and informed and assisting them in their research related to investing in your product or service.

Although we've covered value in this book in other areas, remember that the main difference in developing and sharing your LTKTS is that you share one resource rather than multiple. In other words, you select one piece of value to share with your list of prospects you are nurturing, not multiple different pieces of value.

Here are some examples, keeping in mind what you select should be relevant for all of those on your long-term keep-in-touch list:

- A quarterly report on the state of the industry
- A monthly or quarterly newsletter
- An annual or biannual report covering key aspects of the industry
- A recent and relevant study that you share a perspective on
- A recent case study of a client or customer win
- A monthly or quarterly interview with a recognized executive in the industry
- A monthly or quarterly webinar or virtual presentation

You can vary these value assets (e.g., an annual report + a quarterly webinar) or stick with one (e.g., our quarterly outlook on trends in the commercial insurance industry), setting the frequency that makes the most sense for you. Just ensure that what you share is focused on providing value, insights, help, support, perspectives, etc., to your prospects. In other words, it's useful information.

4. What methods of delivery should you use to stand out?

Your keep-in-touch strategy is different from regular prospecting in that your goal is to remain "top of mind" and continue to build trust with your prospects to the extent that when they need your product or service, you will be the go-to resource. Therefore, your delivery method should be easy for you to execute and have staying power with the prospect. Even if it is jam-packed with value, sending an email does not have staying power because it quickly gets pushed to the bottom of the prospect's inbox as new emails arrive.

Here are some examples of delivery methods that have staying power:

- Regular mail (i.e., a special newsletter, birthday, holiday card, or postcard).
- Courier package (i.e., a special report, annual report, "state of the industry" article).
- Video message (i.e., provide an insight, share an interview, share a presentation).

Your goal is to create something you can easily replicate to send to dozens or even hundreds of prospects, while also standing out from the daily information and noise your prospects are receiving.

5. How do you simplify this outreach for yourself, minimizing your time investment?

Depending on what you decide to share, there are many options to simplify your outreach and reduce your labor intensity, for example:

- Use a direct mail company
- Hire a video editor
- Use a student from a local college or university
- Engage a virtual assistant

Keep in mind that your goal is to provide a resource that is applicable to all, stands out from anything else they receive, and is easy for you to replicate.

You consider creating something for each industry if you sell into multiple industries.

Now that we've discussed your prospect nurture system, why it's important, and what you can share, let's discuss the steps to develop your own nurture process.

16.2 LONG-TERM PROSPECT NURTURING STEPS

The steps in your long-term prospect nurture system should be as follows:

1. Identify your criteria for who becomes a long-term prospect (i.e., at what point do you move someone from a regular prospect to your nurture process?)
2. What different sectors, industries, or groups of prospects do you pursue? Create different categories for long-term prospects to allow you to customize what they receive.
3. Make a list of the different values you can provide and decide if you will choose a single-value asset (e.g., a physically mailed "annual report") or a mix of different values (e.g., a special report, an invitation to an event, a holiday greeting card).
4. Map out a calendar of when you will share this value – scheduling time before the "delivery date" to give yourself enough time to coordinate, develop, and/or deliver. Put this date in your calendar and schedule accordingly.
5. Identify how you will track those you move to your nurture list. Options include a spreadsheet or Google Doc, or, in some instances, it might be possible to make a special note or highlight them in your CRM software (if you do this, make sure you can easily pull a list of these long-term nurture prospects from your CRM).
6. Test your assumptions on what prospects will value. Develop one of the value assets you've identified and begin sharing it with new prospects as something you provide them in early meetings. Ask for their feedback on whether it is useful, helpful, or beneficial.
7. Develop your list to nurture, finalize it, and send your first nurture asset. In your calendar, schedule the subsequent development and sending of additional assets.

16.3 ADDITIONAL TIPS FOR LAUNCHING YOUR PROSPECT NURTURE SYSTEM

Here are some additional tips to consider with your prospect nurture system to ensure it is effective in helping you remain in front of long-term ideal prospects while keeping your efforts simple.

1. Make sure to include your contact information (e.g., a business card, a printed version of your email signature) with each asset so intrigued prospects can easily reach you.
2. If you share a report, article, or other print material, add a sticky note, and write a note that highlights what's most important about the information you're sending.
3. Although what you share should be easy to assemble, you should still attempt to personalize it to the extent possible. For example, ensure that whatever you send includes your prospect's name and other pertinent details. The more personalized you can make it (without overwhelming yourself in preparing the information), the better. It should appear as something you put together just for them, even though you may create dozens, if not hundreds, to send.
4. If you do decide to send your value asset via email (e.g., quarterly newsletter, digital report), make sure it stands out from a typical email.
5. Include an invitation to connect with whatever you send. For example, you include a note or something you have printed on the value asset. For instance, in something I sent recently to my nurture list, there was a section that said – "If these challenges plague your sales team, or if you would like to improve your teams' selling skills, reach out to me at xxx@xxx or call ###-####, and let's discuss."
6. Avoid being overly promotional by including sale flyers or discount coupons. Your goal here is to add value, intrigue your prospect, and remain top of mind, not to come off like you're selling commoditized or low-end products (even if you are!).

Now that you've implemented a nurturing process, the last step is determining how long you will continue it. After all, should you attempt to stay in touch with an ideal prospect forever, or is there a better formula for assessing how long is long enough?

16.4 WHEN TO LET GO OF A PROSPECT

Many years ago, I had a small team of a dozen salespeople working for me. As we brought on new team members, one of the biggest complaints I heard was that the CRM system wasn't handy. We had thousands of contacts in the system. However, a good majority of the contacts were either out of date (i.e., they had been entered years ago, with no contact made since), contained incorrect or insufficient information (i.e., the email address was wrong, a misspelled name), or were no longer active, having moved onto a different company, role, or, in one instance, was dead!

After some internal discussions, we decided a full review and scrub of the CRM information was in order. We set about identifying what needed to be reviewed, proper formatting for each contact, rules around when to remove a contact from the CRM, etc.

Upon sharing this information with the sales team, one of my long-time team members, Stacey, called me. With a somewhat upset tone, she asked, "Do you realize what you're asking us to do with these CRM clean-up instructions?" I remained silent. "You're asking me to take literally hundreds of connections that I've added into the CRM, whom I've been painstakingly pursuing for years, and simply delete them." I continued to remain silent, Stacey continued. "All of my work to find, pursue, and build relationships with these prospective clients, and you want me to delete them. What a complete waste of my time. Why did we enter prospects in the first place if we intended to delete them within a few years?"

You may be unable to sense from what I share, but Stacey was not pleased with our plan. She was one of our longest-tenured team members and had put a lot of effort into prospecting for leads and updating those leads in the CRM. The problem was, however, that some of those leads were nearing ten years old and didn't show much or any activity during the last few years. In her defense, however, Stacey repeatedly brought on new clients, some of whom she worked on for years and years.

Stacey's point, however, sticks with me today: When is the right time to let go of a prospect and move on to someone new? This question is often one that my clients and colleagues like to debate. After all, it isn't easy to maintain your full attention on prospects you've been pursuing for months, or even years, without a hint of acknowledgment from them. But here's something you might not have considered: Every prospect you pursue may need what you sell, but they may not need it right now. In other words, it might be urgent for you to want to contact a new prospect, build a relationship, and then sell them your product or service, but that doesn't mean they need or desire to engage with you now. Let me give you some examples:

- You sell commercial insurance, and your prospect already has a provider of insurance they are happy with.
- You sell geomatic services, and your prospect already uses your competitor, with whom they have a long-term relationship with no issues or complaints.
- You sell accounting services, and your prospect already has an accountant they've worked with for nearly ten years.
- You sell mining equipment, and your prospect has been purchasing similar equipment from your competitor without any issues or complaints.
- You sell manufactured components, and your prospect purchases them from a local company that has been supplying them since they launched their business.

In all these examples, the prospects you reach out to most likely already have a relationship with another supplier, vendor, partner, or contractor, which falls into one of three categories:

1. The existing relationship is sufficient, and the supplier's or vendor's performance or product is acceptable. Making a change would require time and effort from your prospect to investigate, and unless they recognize a significant return on their time invested, they are unlikely to invest time in doing so.
2. The existing relationship is strong, possibly even personal, and the supplier or vendor's performance is excellent. Your prospect would not currently consider making a change. It would take a major mistake or error on the part of their current provider to even consider making a change.
3. The existing relationship with the supplier or vendor is weak, and there have been some recent problems with quality, service, errors, etc. Your prospect has considered looking for a new source (i.e., a new supplier or vendor) and is open to listening to what you have to say.

As a result, you generally have a one in three chance (or 33%) that they will respond to your outreach when they deem it's time to do so. Read that sentence again. In other words, if you've attempted to connect with a prospect, why would you give up after a fixed period? Instead, your goal should remain at the top of your mind as a helpful resource and valuable, trusted advisor that your prospect can rely on. By using a nurturing process correctly, you remain in touch with the other 66% of prospects who may need your services or products.

Back to the original question: when should you let go of a prospect? I would suggest your Nurture Process consist of two categories:

Category 1: Recently completed your initial outreach with no response. Move into a quarterly nurture process where you provide something of value every quarter.

Category 2: Prospects who've been in Group 1 for 24 months move to a biannual nurture process, where they remain in perpetuity. The caveat here is that you should spend time each year flushing out the list for everyone in Group 2. For example, people will retire, leave the industry, change jobs, etc. If they change jobs, you may start them back at the original prospect outreach, as their circumstances and relationships will have changed.

Next, let's finalize all the components of your Unstoppable Sales^{SM} Prospecting System and start implementing the steps to generate a flood of new prospects for you!

UNSTOPPABLE SALES PROSPECTING SYSTEM ACTION STEP

How do you nurture your prospects today? What changes, improvements, or steps can you introduce to develop an easy-to-manage system for staying top of mind? What different examples of value will you share that will be most relevant to your prospects?

17

Build Your Unstoppable Sales^{SM} Prospecting System

Whether you realize it or not, if you've been completing each of the chapter exercises, you now have all the ingredients you need to build your prospecting system! Now we get to the good part: putting your Unstoppable Sales^{SM} Prospecting System into action!

This chapter contains three sections for ease of reading. Each section includes a brief overview of the steps and the specific steps you'll need to take to build and implement your Unstoppable Sales^{SM} Prospecting System. If you don't understand a step or are unsure how to proceed, revisit the table of contents, find the chapter where we previously discussed the component of your Unstoppable Sales^{SM} Prospecting System, and revisit it to ensure you have all the ingredients to implement.

Let's begin with a quick overview. First, we will compile various value assets that you'll use to earn the attention of your ideal prospects. With these identified and developed, the next step will be to work through the core steps to getting your system ready for launch. Lastly, we'll identify the cadence with which you'll use your system to achieve a steady and reliable number of new prospects. If you are ready to get started, let's jump in!

17.1 CREATE YOUR VALUE ASSETS

We discussed value assets in Chapter 3 and then again in Chapter 16. Briefly, these are what you share with a prospect that the prospect might find valuable. The importance of these different assets is threefold:

DOI: 10.4324/9781003604457-22

1. You need to have something to share while you pursue a prospect that addresses questions they may have now or in the future about the product or service you sell.
2. These assets must provoke our prospects (if we expect them to give us their time) by sharing a unique or different perspective from what they would typically hear from our competition.
3. The value we share should satisfy individual communication preferences and consist of various formats for the prospect to consume the information, including visual, audible, and kinesthetic.

With this in mind, let's work through the seven steps to developing your value assets.

17.2 SHAWN'S SEVEN STEPS TO DEVELOPING YOUR VALUE ASSETS

1. Interview existing, past, and potential clients, customers, and prospects to learn what questions, concerns, fears, or problems they have related to your product or service.
2. Determine how you can best answer these questions and share insights related to the feedback you receive. For example, can you provide a report on the state of the sector or industry, free samples, a trial period, testimonials of happy clients or customers, an assessment that provides insights, etc.?
3. Identify the best formats to share the information you believe your prospects will consume (i.e., a printed report you mail, a virtual demonstration, a PDF of testimonials for sharing).
4. How will you share these resources? Can you send some via physical mail, email, social media message, etc.?
5. At what points in your prospecting outreach might you share these resources, and in what order? For example, you might physically mail a report and then begin your outreach via telephone. After you make initial contact, email a PDF including various testimonials.
6. How will you validate the impact of your valuable assets? Do you ask specific questions during the prospecting process to confirm their value? When will you ask for this feedback?

7. Schedule in your calendar a time annually (or more frequently if you prefer) to review your value assets, make improvements or updates, or develop new assets.

Believe it or not, developing your assets is one of the most challenging parts of building your system. It takes creativity, effort, and patience to create assets that are provocative and useful to your prospects, prompting them to want to engage with you. For this reason, you'll need to set aside some focus time to obtain feedback, think through, and then develop your value assets.

To assist with this process, let me give you some examples of my value assets in hopes they spark some ideas for you. Remember that the assets I use appeal to my prospects and may not be relevant to you. For example, my prospects include association executives (who seek out experts to speak at their events), CEOs and Sales Executives (who seek out someone to improve their teams' sales skills through training or workshops), and Sales Leaders (who seek a coach to help them improve their leadership skills and the strength of their sales team).

Here are just a few examples of the value assets I'm currently sharing with these prospects:

Books: My prospects consistently seek ideas on new ways to sell, lead, and support their sales teams. For this reason, I repeatedly write books (e-books and published books), as they provide both a physical asset I can mail or hand to a prospect and a digital version I can email or send via social messaging. For example, my seminal book, *The Unstoppable Sales Machine*, is a resource anyone in sales will find valuable, from CEOs to Sales Leaders and Professionals. Alternatively, my book *The Unstoppable Sales Team* is designed for sales executives and leaders to learn how to be more effective as sales leaders.

Testimonials: I have testimonials that address different scenarios my prospects encounter (e.g., looking for someone to motivate my sales team vs. looking for someone to help my team introduce skills to sell based on value). These are captured in various formats, including written and video, and can be shared in physical mail (send a printed laminated copy) or digital form (sent via email or social media).

Assessments: For anyone seeking to assess their current performance or to identify what changes or improvements to make to improve their team's performance, there are assessments both on my website at www.shawncasemore.com/assessment and as digital files. These assessments provide feedback on commonly asked questions and direct the prospect to a one-to-one conversation to assess whether I can support them in improving their sales performance.

With your value assets now developed, let's review the ten core steps to build your Unstoppable Sales^{SM} Prospecting System.

The Ten-Step Unstoppable Sales^{SM} Prospecting System

There are ten steps to follow when developing your prospecting system. Before we jump to the steps, I guess that if you picked up this book, you are in one of three categories regarding improving your prospecting system, namely:

Category 1: Keep your existing prospecting system and make minor improvements. You already have a prospecting system that works very well and consistently brings in qualified prospects. You are searching for new ideas, techniques, or strategies to improve your work.

Category 2: Modify portions of your existing prospecting system. Your current prospecting system works but isn't consistently bringing you the qualified leads you desire. You want to improve aspects of your prospecting system but don't intend to start from scratch.

Category 3: You have no prospecting system in place at present. You picked up this book because you want to design and launch a prospecting system based on what you learned here.

If you fall into this last category, you will review and complete each step as outlined below. Alternatively, if you fall into category 2 or 3, then my suggestion is that you review each of the steps below first, then compare what you are currently doing (in your prospecting) against each step to determine how you might introduce, improve, or make adjustments to build your Unstoppable Sales^{SM} Prospecting System. We all tend to overestimate the success of what we are doing and underestimate the level of success we can achieve. So even if you fall into the last two categories, don't skim through or jump past these steps. Take your time to review and challenge yourself as to what needs to change or should change.

Ten Steps to Develop Your Unstoppable Sales^{SM} Prospecting System

1. Identify and segment the different prospects you pursue:
   a. What industries or sectors are they in?
   b. What is the company's size (by revenue or employees) for each sector?
   c. What are the titles and responsibilities for each sector?
   d. What are the priorities and challenges for each (by title and sector)?
   e. What are their other interests, values, or hobbies?
2. Identify the best methods to reach your ideal prospects directly (minimum of three):
   a. Phone – desk, cellular, or both
   b. Email – office or personal
   c. LinkedIn (or other social platforms) – direct message or InMail
   d. Direct mail – office address or home address
   e. Text message and/or WhatsApp – business cell or personal cell
   f. Networking – events and associations
3. Identify the best indirect methods to reach your ideal prospects
   a. Referral strategy – multiple mutual connections on LinkedIn or known
   b. Power Partner Network – easy access to others who also sell to your prospects
   c. Association involvement – associations with plenty of face-to-face networking
   d. Speak-to-sell – opportunities to speak in front of your ideal prospect
4. Identify the value assets for each segment that are provocative and useful, for example:
   a. Special reports or annual reports
   b. Free samples, trial periods, test drives, consultations
   c. Assessments (that share best practices)
   d. Demonstrations (that engage the prospect as part of the process)
   e. Explainer videos
5. Develop your touchpoint outreach strategy (minimum of 16) and scripts, for example:
   a. TP#1: Email (e.g. share a relevant statistic and ask a provocative question).

    b. TP#2: Courier a special report (with a note referencing the earlier email).

    c. TP#3: Leave a voice message to confirm the report arrived (offer to discuss).

    d. Etc., etc.

6. Prepare your initial meeting agenda, script, and presentation (if applicable), for example:

    a. What are your minimum and maximum goals for the meeting?

    b. What questions should you ask?

    c. How will you start the meeting? How will you end the meeting?

    d. What relevant examples and/or stories will you share?

    e. What samples, demonstrations, slides, etc., are needed?

7. Develop your follow-up strategy for each prospect interaction, for example:

    a. After the initial response from your prospect

    b. After initial contact with your prospect

    c. After your initial meeting with the prospect

    d. After any subsequent meetings with the prospect

    e. After you issue a prospect proposal or quote

8. Develop your Prospect Nurture System (PNS), for example:

    a. What are your criteria for moving someone to your PNS?

    b. How will you track your prospects in your nurture program?

    c. What frequency will you share information with these prospects?

    d. What value assets will you develop to share?

    e. How will you share this information (i.e., direct mail, email)?

9. Finalize your indirect prospecting methods (identified in step three), for example:

    a. What are the indirect activities you will engage in to connect with prospects?

    b. Which priority will you engage in these activities (do them one at a time)?

    c. How will you measure the success of your involvement (what are the criteria)?

    d. How long will you engage before you can assess the method's effectiveness?

10. Launch your Unstoppable Sales^{SM} Prospecting System!
    a. Schedule time to work through the steps above
    b. Set a date to launch your system (your goal!)
    c. Identify your measures of success (i.e., the number of prospect meetings per week)
    d. Set aside time weekly to review your progress and make any adjustments
    e. Set aside time quarterly to make improvements to your system (based on your results)
    f. Keep going!!

I've included the above steps in a worksheet for you to use. To access it, visit unstoppablesalesprospecting.com to download the worksheet and design your Unstoppable Sales^{SM} Prospecting System.

If you focus on them without distractions, working through these steps will take you one to two days, if you have already developed your value assets (which is why I placed it as the step before your system).

With your system designed, the next question is to determine your prospecting cadence. Let's discuss that next.

17.3 SETTING YOUR PROSPECTING SYSTEM CADENCE

With your methods, content, and process now identified, let's revisit setting the frequency or cadence with which you'll need to prospect for the best results. I shared earlier in this book about my Accelerated Outreach Touchpoint Timing and the many reasons for its effectiveness. Now it's time to put it into practice. Here is an example:

Shawn's Accelerated Outreach Touchpoint Timing:

TP#1: Day 1
TP#2: Day 8
TP#3: Day 14
TP#4: Day 19
TP#5: Day 23
TP#6: Day 26
TP#7: Day 28
TP#8: Day 29

This approach is intended to slowly warm up your prospect, which is how a normal trusting relationship is built.

As a quick aside, whether you follow my approach or not, you should never send a message to your prospect that says, "This will be the last time you hear from me." Do not, under any circumstances, do this! It's a great example of what I mentioned above, where a sales professional has read and attempted to replicate something online. Did you know that the origins of this come from online marketers who, after attempting to sell a product, course, or service, set up a series of email automation designed to get people to buy something by a certain deadline (i.e., Friday at midnight), after which they typically launch another new product?

You are not an online marketer, and you (likely) would have no intention of dropping that prospect from your list (if you do, then you should reconsider and revisit our earlier discussion on nurturing your prospects). Worse yet, when you send this kind of message, your prospect typically thinks, "Great! Now I don't have to hear from them again!"

In designing your touchpoint strategy using my Accelerated Outreach Approach, once you've reached touchpoint #8, you'll need to consider whether you should start the cycle again or move them to your Prospect

Accelerated Touchpoint Strategy Frequency

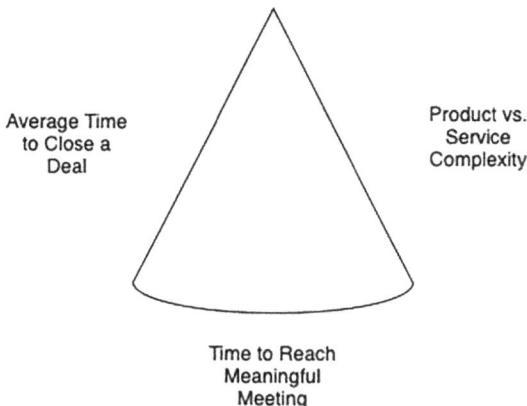

DIAGRAM 17.1
Accelerated Touchpoint Strategy Frequency.

Nurture Program. To assess the best approach, you'll want to consider the speed to sale of the specific industry or sector you sell into, which will inform when to move to nurturing your prospect, and the best frequency of your nurturing. In other words, a longer sales cycle might result in extending the development of a nurture program that starts biweekly and then transitions to monthly and quarterly over time. Alternatively, a short sales cycle might result in your relaunching your Accelerated Touchpoint strategy a second time before moving to a quarterly nurture program. Diagram 17.1 identifies three considerations that will help you make this decision.

17.4 FACTORS TO DETERMINE FREQUENCY OF PROSPECT NURTURING

1. **What You Sell**: Whether you sell a product or service will determine the frequency of your outreach. For example, selling a service focuses more heavily on building trust than on proving the quality of the product. To be clear, you need to build trust in both scenarios; however, a service is more focused on demonstrating the expertise of your company and the people within it.

2. **Time to Close the Sale**: Consider the time it takes to close the average deal (sometimes referred to as the frequency with which your prospect replenishes your product or service). If you sell a service with a set contract term or expensive software or equipment, it's unlikely a prospect will make a change quickly. As a result, spread your prospecting out over an extended period (e.g., one year).

3. **Who Makes the Buy Decision**: If you sell a product or service that is typically sourced by someone in Procurement or Purchasing, your prospecting time will be extended compared to selling directly to your end-user. In the first scenario, procurement or purchasing will have a set schedule in which they intend to review sources of supply, whereas in the second scenario you can build trust and influence a prospect to make a change immediately.

You'll want to consider other factors that may be specific to your sector. However, these are the most common that impact prospecting and nurture duration.

Once you've assessed the best frequency of touchpoints and nurturing, you must ensure you have time set aside to prospect (an often-overlooked aspect of prospecting, with many sales professionals attempting to squeeze in their prospecting rather than plan for it strategically). Here are some considerations to ensure you have sufficient time to succeed.

17.5 HOW TO IDENTIFY THE TIME REQUIRED TO PROSPECT

Step 1 – Identify Leads: Depending on how you identify leads (i.e., research online using Google, association member lists, LinkedIn Sales Navigator), you'll need to set aside time to identify these new leads. For example, you might set aside time each week or month to research or use tools like ZoomInfo, Apollo.io, or LinkedIn Sales Navigator, which can feed you leads if you set up filters and lists to manage accordingly.

Suggested Strategy: LinkedIn Sales Navigator lets you view 2500 prospects across 100 pages. If you use LinkedIn, you can build your initial list here and then download outside of LinkedIn to search or upload to other platforms. It also makes it easy to manage connections and messaging on the platform, which can be more labor-intensive than email.

Step 2 – Time for Outreach: To this point, you've identified your primary methods of reaching out to and connecting with prospects. Depending on your selected methods, the time required to make connections will be something you need to plan for. For example, you've identified networking at association events as a primary lead-generation tool. In that case, you'll need to schedule meetings into your calendar and plan time before and after the event for outreach and follow-up. If you've decided to speak at events, you'll need to set aside time to research relevant events where you can talk and reach out to inquire about the opportunity. If you are making calls or using direct mail or email, again, you'll need to set aside time to accomplish these tasks.

Suggested Strategy: Block time in your calendar weekly on the days and times you typically are at your desk or office. For example, you can use Monday from 10 am to 2 pm to identify leads, organize meetings, and conduct outreach before upcoming events. Then, plan Tuesday and Wednesday for travel days, then Thursday as a buffer day (to draft proposals and meet with prospects), and then

Friday for updating notes in CRM and developing your lists to pursue the following week.

Step 3 – New Value Assets: Although the demand to develop new value assets won't be as intensive or frequent as the others above, you'll still want to set aside time each quarter, or every six months, to improve upon existing assets or develop new assets. Your goal is to always remain relevant, which means what you share will need to change as market conditions evolve, customer or client relationships change, new testimonials are collected, etc.

Suggested Strategy: Set aside time each quarter (i.e., 1–2 hours) to review your value assets. Identify what's been getting you the most attention (i.e., people are interested) and what's not working. Make any necessary changes, adjustments, or updates, or develop new value assets to continue adding relevant and practical value to your prospects. This exercise also gives you a reason to reach out to prospects who have gone dormant (i.e., "Sue, we haven't spoken in a while, and I thought you'd appreciate this new customer service feature we've introduced for clients.").

Congratulations! You've now assembled all the components to launch your Unstoppable Sales^SM Prospecting System. Now that we've addressed the critical factors influencing the frequency and duration of your prospecting, let's jump into Part Six and discuss some other considerations to ensure your Prospecting System is successful!

UNSTOPPABLE SALES PROSPECTING SYSTEM ACTION STEP

Work through the steps above to develop your Unstoppable Sales^SM Prospecting System. Make sure to visit https://unstoppablesalesprospecting.com for more resources, tools, and templates to assist you.

Part Six

Final Word
Your Prospecting Success
Starts with You

With your Unstoppable Sales^{SM} Prospecting System now in place (or at least under construction), let's discuss a few critical areas you'll want to monitor, as they can tremendously impact your success (or lack thereof) with the system.

When it comes to prospecting with your new system, being consistent, remaining positive, and integrating technology will be three considerations you'll need to make on an ongoing basis. Each of these factors individually plays a vital role in determining your success. Combined, they have the potential to derail you permanently, so read the coming chapters carefully to ensure all your hard work to this point doesn't go to waste.

In the forthcoming chapters, we'll discuss ensuring long-term success by addressing these areas. I also share some insights on changes and future predictions for the sales professional's role and how you can prepare for and capitalize on these changes.

DOI: 10.4324/9781003604457-23

18

Time Mastery

Your Secret Weapon

Let's begin with a quick exercise. Take out your calendar and identify how many hours you have assigned to prospecting this coming week. To be clear, this is the time dedicated to researching new prospects, reaching out to prospects, following up with prospects, and speaking with prospects directly. Once you have noted the number of hours spent on these activities in the coming week, look back at your calendar to identify whether these hours are consistent. The reason you should look back is that it's not uncommon for you to make plans to spend a certain number of hours prospecting each week, only to find those hours quickly consumed doing other less important tasks.

With this information, compare this number to your overall calendar for a percentage of your total time using the formula in Diagram 18.1.

Does your number seem too low to you? Considering all the other meetings and projects on your calendar, you may be happy with it. If you are like most sales professionals, this number will hover around 25% or less of your total time. The question for you to consider is, if prospects are your only source of new business, how much time should you dedicate to prospecting every week?

DOI: 10.4324/9781003604457-24

Time Available to Prospect

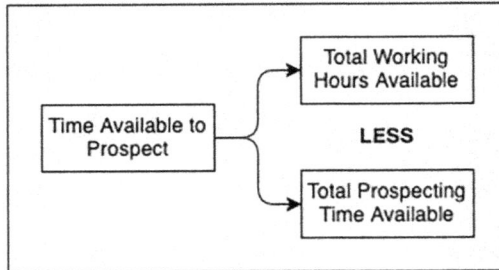

DIAGRAM 18.1
Time Available to Prospect.

18.1 HOW MUCH TIME SHOULD YOU SPEND PROSPECTING?

The more time you spend prospecting, the more prospects you'll generate. This statement is true to some extent, but the reality is that unless you are new to your role, there will be other obligations you have to meet that will absorb some of your prospecting time.

The longer you are in a role often means the less time you have available to prospect. Your initial prospecting time gets absorbed the more customers you close (as they may require some degree of ongoing communication) and the more people in your company that get to know you (and, in turn, pull you into internal meetings). Here are some typical examples of how your non-prospecting time may get absorbed:

- Meetings with your team and your manager
- One-to-one meetings with your manager
- Companywide meetings or town halls
- Meetings with existing clients or customers
- Meetings with other departments or department managers

These meetings can be either preplanned or impromptu, but ultimately, they mean one thing – less time available for you to prospect. These meetings will

How to Calculate Your Ideal Prospecting Time	
1	Annual Target Revenue/Average Revenue Per Sale = # Deals to Close
2	# Deals to Close × Percent Closing Ratio = # Opportunities to Generate
3	# Opportunities to Generate × Lead to # Opportunity Conversion = # Prospects to Pursue
4	# Prospects to Pursue × Average Time Per Prospect = Prospect Time Required

DIAGRAM 18.2
Calculate Prospecting Time Required.

also require increasing communications or interactions, such as responding to or sharing updates with your manager, responding to your existing or past customers, and responding to internal emails.

There is no way for me to know exactly how much time you should spend prospecting since I don't see what you sell, the dynamics of your job, your organization, or the intricacies of your role. However, considering all these variables, you can use a formula to determine how much time you should spend prospecting. It's not an exact science, but it will help determine if you are investing enough time.

To use the formula, you will need access to the following information:

- Your annual sales revenue target
- Your average revenue per sale
- Your closing ratio
- Your conversion rates

Diagram 18.2 outlines these steps in an easy-to-use format to assist you with your own calculations.

18.2 STEPS TO CALCULATE YOUR PROSPECTING TIME

1. Annual Target Sales Revenue/Average Revenue per Sale = Number of Deals to Close
2. Number of Deals to Close/Closing Ratio = Number of Opportunities to Generate

3. Number of Opportunities/Conversion Rate = Number of Prospects to Pursue
4. Number of Prospects/Prospecting Time Per Prospect* = Prospecting Time Required

*Note: This is the average time you take to complete all the touchpoints for each prospect, which can vary depending on several factors, including prospect availability, interruptions while prospecting, etc. For this reason, calculate an average number that you can use in the formula above.

Although the formula is straightforward, there are some additional points you may struggle with. For example, if you are new to sales or working with a company, you may not know your closing ratio, conversion rate, or other formula aspects. If so, speak with your manager or co-workers to understand their averages. Doing so will allow you to set a starting point, which you can adjust by reapplying the formula later.

With your average prospecting time now identified, you can estimate the amount of time required to prospect to meet your targets. You should then schedule this time in your calendar, which brings us to the next critical question for you to answer: When do you prospect?

As with anything else, this question will vary depending on several factors, including the availability of your prospects, time zones for yourself and your prospects, etc. Various factors can affect these times, including your prospect's role, whether they travel for work, whether they work remotely, whether they lead a team or are a solo contributor, and their responsibilities (e.g., lead a team or be a solo contributor). Track your success in connecting with prospects (and that of your peers) and develop your criteria for when it is best to reach them. Use the above as a starting point, but determine your best practices.

18.3 KEEP YOUR PROSPECTING PLANS ON TRACK

As referenced earlier, remaining consistent in your prospecting efforts as you progress is a consistent challenge for most sales professionals. The reasons for being unable to stay consistent vary, but often include:

- Being pulled into unplanned or unexpected meetings
- Getting distracted by scanning social media or web pages while prospecting

- Extended vacations that impact your routine
- Extended absences from work for personal reasons
- New projects or assignments that consume significant time
- Travel schedules that vary from week to week or month to month

Aside from these, most sales professionals lose focus on their commitments because of a lack of results. After all, it isn't easy to remain on track when you aren't experiencing the desired outcomes.

Staying on track with your prospecting schedule, targets, and personal goals is both easy and challenging at the same time. It's easy, for example, to have the desire to remain consistent – after all, that will ensure you retain your job, support your family, and have a sense of accomplishment at the end of the day. Alternatively, staying on track is challenging because life can get in the way.

Since there is no secret formula to share with you, let me provide insights into what top-performing sales professionals repeatedly use to help them stay on track with their commitments.

18.4 SHAWN'S PROSPECTING PLAN COMMITMENT

1. **Set Quantifiable Targets**: Identify your daily, weekly, and monthly prospecting targets (i.e., how many people you will reach out to and follow up with weekly).
2. **Commit Time in Your Calendar**: Block out time in your calendar to complete your prospecting tasks. Book meetings with yourself that include a proper title and agenda (e.g., Monday 9:00 am – 10:00 am: Prospect Research; Monday 10:30 am – 12:00 pm: Prospect Outreach).
3. **Introduce Meaningful Rewards**: What will you reward yourself if you remain on track with your targets (i.e., if you make the number of phone calls and meet your target, what's the reward?). Go for a walk outside, grab a Starbucks coffee, call your spouse, etc. Small rewards give us something to look forward to once we complete the task.
4. **Add Buffer Time**: You'll notice in my example of a time schedule in #2 above that I left a 30-minute window between activities. I refer to this as buffer time, which you would use to screen and respond to any urgent emails or text messages, then engage in whatever reward you've chosen, such as grabbing a coffee at a Starbucks close by.

5. **Communicate Your Plan**: Tell everyone about your prospecting targets and your committed time. Tell your boss, your co-workers, and even customers when you aren't available because you have a previous commitment. With your boss or co-workers, you can tell them you are prospecting; however, if customers or clients ask for this time, simply let them know you have a previous commitment.

Prospecting can be a double-edged sword. The real reward we seek is prospects who respond to our outreach. Unfortunately, you won't see the results you desire if you don't remain consistent and on track with your prospecting plan! John F. Kennedy once said, "We must use time as a tool, not a couch!" Use your time as a tool by consistently putting in the work, and you'll achieve the results you seek.

18.5 TIME IS YOUR COMPETITIVE ADVANTAGE

In addition to having a prospecting plan that you are committed to and remain consistent with, you'll need to manage one other consideration closely: your calendar.

We discussed this above. However, it's important to highlight just how important managing your calendar is if you want to succeed with your prospecting. Top performers I've met and interviewed over the years are almost militant about how they spend their time. If something isn't on their calendar or arrives without their consent (i.e., an unexpected meeting invitation), then it doesn't happen. Working with these people can be interesting, as they may sometimes seem uncollaborative or less than helpful; however, what they are is hyper-focused on finding and closing their next opportunity.

I've never been a fan of being overly obsessive about managing my own time; however, protecting one's time (and calendar) is such a common characteristic of top sales performers that I repeatedly hold myself to it. If I can manage a hectic work travel schedule, client workload, book writing, and busy home life, then I'm confident you can, too. It just takes commitment.

Now, you may have a personality that enables you to be militant with your time while still being cordial with others, in which case managing your time and calendar likely isn't an issue. For the rest of you who may desire to be more collaborative and a little less militant, like me, here are some tips for you to consider protecting your time and your calendar.

18.6 SHAWN'S RULES TO PROTECT YOUR TIME

Prepare Your Mind: You may not be able to jump directly from a task or meeting into prospecting. Often, it takes a few minutes to clear our minds and prepare for the next task, so give yourself ten minutes of time at the beginning of your prospecting to do something you enjoy. Whether that's scanning social media, playing a quick game of Angry Birds, getting a fresh cup of coffee, talking to a co-worker, etc.

Enable Yourself to Focus: Close your door, put on headphones, turn on music, etc. Whatever helps you focus on what's in front of you, make sure you include it in your prospecting routine.

Communicate Your Schedule: If others know you are prospecting, they are more likely to avoid bothering you (if you've communicated the importance of not being disturbed during this time), so take steps to remind people you can't be distracted, such as printing a sign to hang on your door, sharing a copy of your calendar with time blocked out, or simply communicating when you won't be available during a daily or weekly team meeting.

Eliminate Online Distractions: It's easy to close your door in an office, but it's not so easy to turn off your phone or email notifications. But you must do that if you want to use your prospecting time effectively.

Time Yourself: Our focus is typically only at its strongest for a maximum of 30 minutes. So, plan your tasks in 30-minute increments and give yourself a five-minute break in between. You can use a timer to help yourself stay on track. If you use your phone, ensure all notifications, buzzers, dings, and red lights are turned off so that all that shows on your screen is the timer itself.

It may seem like I'm repeating myself with some of these tips and strategies, and to some degree, that might be true. But I can't emphasize enough how you – your focus, time, and energy – are your greatest competitive advantage when it comes to prospecting. Stay focused, hold yourself accountable, and reward yourself, and you'll be a top-performing sales prospector in no time!

**UNSTOPPABLE SALES PROSPECTING
SYSTEM ACTION STEP**

How diligent are you with managing your time? What else can you introduce to minimize distractions and focus your energy during the time you block for prospecting? Try at least two new strategies from those listed above.

19

The Future of Sales Prospecting

I don't consider myself a futurist, so my predictions on the future of sales prospecting are predicated on my observations and insights gleaned from my network of colleagues and companies that continue to innovate new selling methods.

At the time of this writing, artificial intelligence (AI) is the predominant influence on prospecting and sales in general. However, other technologies are rapidly advancing in addition to AI, although they aren't receiving as much attention. So, I'll share with you below the emerging technologies and their influence on us as sales professionals and how we prospect.

How Prospecting Will Evolve in the Years Ahead

Let's begin with something that might not be obvious but will tremendously influence how sales prospecting evolves. The demographics of our buyers, those prospects we pursue, are changing, which means how we contact them, build trust with them, and develop relationships will evolve. Let me share an example of what I'm referring to.

When I began my first official sales job in the 1990s, you heard me say that email was in its infancy, as was the Internet, and there were no social media channels. Prospects relied heavily on sales professionals, such as me, to help educate and inform them about the products or services they would purchase. They still did "research" before they bought, but their network of peers, colleagues, and existing sales professionals with whom they had a relationship provided the research. As a result, it was much easier to get a meeting with a customer, client, or even a prospect.

We've discussed methods to prospect today and shared various studies that have found prospects are researching before they buy (which isn't new per above). However, much of that research is online. Do prospects

DOI: 10.4324/9781003604457-25

today still take meetings with sales professionals, speak with their peers, or meet up with colleagues at association events to do research? Yes, they do. However, those who do are typically of an older generation and are practicing methods of research that they've used earlier in their careers and for which they have comfort in using. To give you an example, consider from your own experience whether someone who is a prospect today in their fifties or sixties would be more willing to meet with you in person than a prospect in their late twenties. The short answer is yes. However, this isn't to say a younger prospect wouldn't want to meet in person; however, many would prefer to meet virtually, and if they do meet in person, the format of the meeting, the agenda, etc., would all be different (e.g., a shorter meeting at Starbucks).

As your prospects' demographics change, so will their preferences for how and when they connect with sales. Your age and preferences will, therefore, need to evolve to meet the demographic you sell to. For example, if you are in your late twenties and are pursuing a prospect in their late fifties, recognize that how they prefer to communicate and interact with you may differ from your preferences.

Since this can impact your Unstoppable Sales^SM Prospecting System, and considering you are likely selling to people of all ages, here are a few considerations to ensure that how you connect with prospects evolves with their preferences.

19.1 STEPS TO MONITOR THE EVOLUTION OF YOUR PROSPECTS

1. During every prospect meeting, ask your prospect the following questions:
   • How did they learn of you, your company, and its products or services?
   • What communication channels do they prefer to communicate on?
   • What would have made this initial interaction more valuable for them?
2. Track which channels successfully connect with prospects (e.g., Are more prospects responding on LinkedIn or via email?). Adjust your system accordingly.

3. Give your prospects options regarding how you meet (e.g., "Would you prefer to meet in person or via Teams?").

4. Based on their feedback, test new methods of connecting with prospects. For example, if many prospects prefer to text using WhatsApp, test the application as part of your earlier outreach.

5. Monitor your competitors' methods of connecting and meeting with prospects. Be observant during prospect meetings about whether they've interacted with your competitors (e.g., sometimes there may be brochures or other communication you'll see lying around). You can also monitor your competitor's LinkedIn profiles and investigate how their companies use various channels to drive new leads (e.g., are they running ads on LinkedIn).

As we've discussed, if you are using your Unstoppable Sales^{SM} Prospecting System, you already have thinking time in your calendar. Use this time to consider what you've observed, learned, or heard about new ways to connect or interact with prospects, and then do your testing.

A quick warning. Thousands of companies will tell you they have the secret formula to help you succeed in prospecting, from new software to apps to a "team of appointment setters." Be very careful who you listen to for the following reasons:

• Most companies will tell you that their solution is the best to entice you to invest in their product or service. Do your research before you test anything out.

• As a sales professional, you have a reputation to uphold, so the last thing you'll want to do is invest in something that will annoy your prospects. I've seen sales professionals invest in automation to support their outreach, only to have their names or, worse yet, their email addresses get labeled as spam or blocked altogether.

• You have limited time to prospect, so spending that precious time setting up a new piece of software or testing an unproven method of outreach is cutting into your time generating new prospects.

By all means, test things out to determine their impact, but be careful how much time and energy you invest. Above all, monitor the effects of anything you test closely. The old saying goes, "You only get one chance to make a good first impression."

19.2 TECHNOLOGY OPTIONS TO ACCELERATE YOUR PROSPECTING EFFORTS

The influence technology adoption is having on sales is profound. If you were to tell me in my early days of selling that text messages would replace in-person conversations or virtual meetings would replace in-person meetings, I wouldn't have believed you.

As you know, most of these technology applications are old news, but think of the evolution of the last decade alone. The real impact of technology on sales is understanding how quickly technology and its adoption are evolving. This book would be of no use if we didn't address the technology that is impacting sales prospecting; however, recognize that as soon as this is published, there may be a chance some of the information is out of date, so for this reason I'll do my best to discuss emerging technologies and their impact as of the time of this writing.

19.3 ADVANCING TECHNOLOGY AND ITS INFLUENCE ON SALES PROSPECTING

Artificial Intelligence (AI): AI is advancing quickly. From its inception as a tool to scan vast amounts of information with breakneck speed, it's evolving in ways no one expected. Sales professionals today are having great success using various AI software to perform strategic activities such as lead scoring and forecasting to administrative tasks such as perfecting an email outreach script or better language for a pitch deck.

The future of AI and its applications in sales are seemingly endless, with generative AI being the current focus for sales. With generative AI, new content in various formats, including audio, video, text, or images, can be developed based on learning from large datasets. The most significant advantages of generative AI in sales are learning from previous customer or client data and providing proactive prompts to sales professionals, such as suggestions on quick-win deals or recommendations on copy for outreach emails. Generative AI is incorporated into many CRM platforms and will continue to emerge as one of the most helpful technologies for sales professionals who prospect.

AI is influencing how we prospect and the role of the sales professional; however, other advancing technologies are becoming useful tools in the prospecting process.

Virtual Reality and Augmented Reality

Augmented Reality (AR) and Virtual Reality (VR) are having an increasing impact on sales. Often referred to as Immersive Reality, there are a growing number of applications of both AR and VR that you have likely experienced, possibly without even knowing it.

AR is an environment that is real yet has been enhanced or augmented in some way. VR, on the other hand, is an entirely virtual environment.

For example, real estate professionals have long offered virtual tours of homes they are selling. Additionally, you may have noticed recently that Amazon now offers you the opportunity to point your phone camera at your feet and view what a new pair of shoes would look like on your feet, a great example of AR.

In the B2B space, I have one client who is using VR headsets to allow prospective customers to view the layouts of new buildings they are considering purchasing. Another client uses AR to assist in their safety training programs.

Both AR and VR are advancing in applications and functionality. For example, AR and VR are now being integrated with artificial intelligence, which can analyze a wide range of data to create virtual objects and scenarios. This can ensure that users, your prospective customers, have a better experience.

If what you sell can be enhanced by providing your prospects with an experiential interaction, then AR or VR is likely something you'll want to consider.

Machine Learning

The other rapidly advancing technology influencing sales prospecting is machine learning. The most common example is chatbots, often found on company websites. These interact with external visitors to a website, historically facilitating a direct connection between sales and technical support to "chat" and answer questions.

More recently, however, chatbots have expanded their use to provide information, answers to questions, and even suggestions of products or services for the customer to purchase. In this way, chatbots are evolving to become machine customers designed with pre-programmed criteria to make purchase decisions on behalf of a customer.

In brief, these are software-driven entities connected to the Internet designed to interact with businesses and people to perform tasks, gather information, and facilitate transactions.

Common examples of machine customers you may have encountered include:

- Chatbots,
- virtual assistants,
- autonomous vehicles, and
- smart appliances.

If, for example, you've ever asked Amazon Alexa to purchase something for you using your Amazon account, then you've used a machine customer! Alexa uses your payment information and the rules you provide (e.g., to purchase a specific product) from Amazon. In this way, Alexa acts as an Amazon customer.

At present, machine customers can only purchase certain items based on predefined rules created by humans. An example you might have encountered is the Amazon Dash Replenishment Service, which uses smart shelves in homes or offices to trigger reorders of consumable products once a certain threshold is reached.

AI is expected to heavily influence the evolution of machine customers. In this scenario, machine customers will optimize the choices or selections provided using AI and then make the buy decision. Examples you may have seen include robot trading and autonomous vehicles.

Other areas of technology influence and will influence your prospecting. If selected strategically, they can assist in improving the effectiveness and efficiency of your Unstoppable Sales^{SM} Prospecting System.

19.4 YOUR LONG-TERM SUCCESS IN SALES

To close, I wanted to share something with you that will profoundly influence your ability to prospect: your mindset.

As we've covered in this book, our prospects, their preferences, technology, and the global economy are all evolving and changing. There's a saying, often attributed to the Greek philosopher Heraclitus, that, "the only constant in life is change." The only guarantee in your sales career is change. However, given the continued changes in behaviors and advancing technology, what's important is that you develop a proven system to prospect, one that you can modify and improve upon over time but that provides you with a steady stream of prospects. My intention with this book is to share with you strategies that are working, compiled into a system that you can introduce and use to balance your career in sales.

There will be more technology, and with each new technology will come promises of an easier job. However, don't get distracted by these often-empty promises. Putting your Unstoppable Sales^SM Prospecting System into place will take both focus and effort on your part; however, by introducing a systematic approach to prospecting, coupled with applying the right habits and behaviors, you will achieve results. Your results will in turn provide you with the confidence and motivation to keep going, and that's the formula for long-term success in prospecting. Diagram 19.1 demonstrates how to build the right habits and behaviors.

Let me end by saying this. Sales is one of the most noble and rewarding professions you can have. Get clear on your goals, stick with your system, and keep pushing forward. My goal is to help you achieve success in the

Unstoppable Selling Habits

DIAGRAM 19.1
Unstoppable Selling Habits.

shortest amount of time possible because, frankly, we need more people like you in sales. If you enjoyed this book, pass it along to someone who you think could benefit from it. If you'd like to stay in touch, or you'd like more resources, tips, and strategies to improve your selling success, make sure you visit my website at www.shawncasemore.com and while you are there, sign up to join our Thursday Thrive Community.

References

1. https://en.wikipedia.org/wiki/Frequency_illusion
2. https://en.wikipedia.org/wiki/William_Moulton_Marston
3. https://www.amazon.com/stores/author/B000AP7EBS
4. https://en.wikipedia.org/wiki/Learning_styles
5. https://www.salesforce.com/service/digital-customer-engagement-platform/what-is-customer-engagement/
6. https://www.frontiersin.org/journals/psychology/articles/10.3389/fpsyg.2023.1219945/full
7. https://www.gartner.com/en/newsroom/press-releases/2020-09-15-gartner-says-80-of-b2b-sales-interactions-between-su
8. https://www.gartner.com/en/confirmation/publications/win-more-b2b-sales-deals
9. https://www.gartner.com/en/sales/trends/future-of-sales
10. https://www.zippia.com/advice/cold-calling-statistics/
11. https://www.rainsalestraining.com/blog/infographic-30-sales-prospecting-stats-and-what-they-mean-for-sellers
12. https://outplayhq.com/blog/cold-calling-statistics
13. https://www.gong.io/blog/cold-call-stats/
14. https://fortune.com/2024/02/16/fridays-without-meetings-productivity-focus-flow/
15. https://pipeline.zoominfo.com/sales/cold-sales-voicemails
16. https://cdn2.hubspot.net/hubfs/123161/PDFs/5%20Sales%20Prospecting%20Myths%20Debunked.pdf
17. https://www.nngroup.com/articles/email-newsletters-inbox-congestion/
18. https://sproutsocial.com/glossary/call-to-action-cta/
19. https://www.saleshandy.com/blog/psychology-behind-cold-email-follow-up/
20. https://www.linkedin.com/pulse/important-linkedin-statistics-data-trends-oleksii-bondar-pqlie/
21. https://skrapp.io/blog/linkedin-statistics/
22. https://business.linkedin.com/sales-solutions/sales-navigator
23. https://www.dataaxleusa.com/blog/direct-mail-statistics/
24. https://www.vidyard.com/blog/video-for-abm/
25. https://www.virginmediao2business.co.uk/pdf/insights/reports/movers-index-q4-2023.pdf
26. https://blog.thebrevetgroup.com/21-mind-blowing-sales-stats
27. https://www.intelngin.com/
28. https://www.crossrivertherapy.com/public-speaking-statistics
29. https://www.joerogan.com/
30. https://www.howardstern.com/show/
31. https://www.youtube.com/@ShawnCasemore
32. https://www.superoffice.com/blog/prospecting/
33. https://www.simplypsychology.org/pavlov.html
34. https://www.scientificamerican.com/article/how-long-does-it-really-take-to-form-a-habit/
35. https://positivepsychology.com/3-steps-negativity-bias/

Index

Note: Page numbers in *italics* indicate figures, and page numbers in **bold** indicate tables in the text.

For Product Safety Concerns and Information please contact our EU
representative GPSR@taylorandfrancis.com
Taylor & Francis Verlag GmbH, Kaufingerstraße 24, 80331 München, Germany

www.ingramcontent.com/pod-product-compliance
Lightning Source LLC
Chambersburg PA
CBHW061216220326
41599CB00025B/4663